THE RHYTHM AT THE
HEART OF THE WORLD

Monkey Press is named after the Monkey King in The Journey to the West, the 16th century novel by Wu Chengen. Monkey blends skill, initiative and wisdom with the spirit of freedom, irreverence and mischief.

Also published by Monkey Press:
The Way of Heaven: Neijing Suwen chapters 1 and 2
The Secret Treatise of the Spiritual Orchid: Neijing Suwen chapter 8
The Seven Emotions
The Eight Extraordinary Meridians
The Extraordinary Fu
Essence Spirit Blood and Qi
The Lung
The Kidneys
Spleen and Stomach
The Heart in Ling shu chapter 8
The Liver
Heart Master Triple Heater
A Study of Qi
Yin Yang in Classical Texts
The Essential Woman
Pregnancy and Gestation
Wu Xing: The Five Elements in Chinese Classical Texts
Jing Shen: A Translation of Huainanzi chapter 7

THE RHYTHM AT THE
HEART OF THE WORLD

A translation with commentary of
NEIJING SUWEN CHAPTER 5

Elisabeth Rochat de la Vallée

MONKEY PRESS

© Monkey Press 2011
The Rhythm at the Heart of the World: Neijing suwen chapter 5
Elisabeth Rochat de la Vallée

ISBN 978 1 872468 11 2

All rights reserved. No part of this book may be reproduced
in any form without the written permission of the publisher.

Cover image: Based on the unfolded design from an ornamental bronze
drum. Western Han Dynasty; unearthed in 1965, Dingxian, Hebei.

Translated from the original French by Nora Franglen
Edited by Sandra Hill

www.monkeypress.net
monkey.press@virgin.net

Printed in the UK by MPG Books Group, Bodmin and Kings Lynn

INTRODUCTION

Suwen chapter five is one of the most important texts on the establishment of Chinese medical theory according to the principles of *yin yang* and the five elements. This is the reason why it is called a 'great treatise' (*da lun*) whereas most of the other Suwen chapters are merely called 'treatise' (*lun*).

The primordial *qi*, the single origin of the multiple spreading of life, first manifests itself through the rhythm of *yin yang*. Everything in the universe is understood in terms of *yin yang*, and differentiation is made between the clear, pure and diffuse, and the turbid, heavy and coagulated, and thus heaven and earth appear.

But the reality of the couple is in their relationship. *Yin* or *yang*, as well as heaven or earth, do not exist one without the other; they exist only in and through their relationships and all living beings are formed in and through these relationships.

Each of the 'ten thousand beings', i.e. each of the myriad beings and phenomena which people the universe, owes its advent to a specific gathering of *yin yang qi* between heaven and earth. This specific configuration defines each individual being and thing – its inner organization of life, its nature, its strength and its duration, as well as its affinities with all other beings. The interactions between all beings and phenomena create continual transformations – whose laws and principles may be understood through assessing the *yin yang* nature of each of them.

By observing the natural movements of life, such as the regular sequence of the four seasons, the effects of the *qi* of heaven on earth (creating, for instance, time and weather), human beings are able to recognize the great laws and major cycles operating within the constant interactions between the multiple aggregations of *qi* which constitute all beings. The intelligence which belongs to the human heart/mind allows us to comprehend the beauty and order of heaven and earth, of nature and of the universe.

Once we are able to discern the primordial *yin yang* rhythm in natural phenomena, such as sun and shadow, day and night, heat and cold, activity and rest, an evolution of thought enables us to use *yin yang* as a couple which is not bound to any particular reality, but which represents this double aspect intrinsic to all that exists.

Likewise, when considering the concrete raw materials necessary for their survival (water, fire, wood, metal, earth), human beings created the 'five elements', which are five modes for all activity of *qi*, five processes which organize the five-fold aspect intrinsic to all that exists.

Once the universal relevance of *yin yang* and five elements is well established, the development of knowledge –and even what may be called science – is dependent on them. The template of life is made with *yin yang* and five elements. This means that it is only possible to understand the nature and the functionning of a being or of a phenomenon (or of a series of beings or phenomena) through *yin yang* and the five elements.

In order to understand how a human being functions and to discover the rules for the organization of human life and the human body, the Chinese use the laws, principles, cycles, patterns, models for action and reaction which are shown by *yin yang* and five elements. Their mode of action and interaction is codified in order to be applied to any specific instance.

Consequently, medical knowledge is based on the knowledge of the processes of *yin yang* and the five elements. To improve and refine the way we recognize them in any specific situation of life in a human being, is to build a means for diagnosis which enables an efficient treatment. The treatment will restore the natural order which has been lost, following the precise identification of the disorder.

It may seem childish or foolish to proceed in such a way.

To say that in a human the head is identical to heaven and the feet to earth may appear simplistic. It is the same as to profess that the movements of the fluids in the body are understood by considering the evaporation that makes clouds and the clouds that make rain. We may think that it is simply poetic and imaginative to assert that the liver is identical to the wind, the spring, the east, and to anything belonging to the wood element; we may consider it poetic and creative, but useless and not relevant to a real medical knowledge.

Nevertheless, Suwen chapter 5 claims to establish the basis for an authentic medicine. This is because it is a matter of *qi*. If we understand how the *qi* interact and play together, such an understanding is relevant for any being or phenomenon, because they are all constituted by the same *qi*, and they all share the same origin. They are correlated – associated in corespondances which are not static, but are modes of exchange and relationship, always moving, changing and evolving.

In order to understand the *qi* of the wood element, one has to observe this *qi* in natural phenomena – as the wind, the rising sun, etc; one has to experiment with it in one's own life when the anger is swelling or when the soul overflows with generosity. Thus one can recognize it in others, in a flash of the eye or the bursting out of words, in a skin rash or in a stroke, in spring or juvenile energy. To understand the *qi* of wood is to understand the liver within a human being. What is called 'liver' in Chinese medicine combines all the activities of physiology, psychology and mind, which are made by this wood *qi*.

Suwen chapter 5 conveys how a deep knowedge of *yin yang* and the five elements allows us to understand the way a human being functions, to know the intrinsic organization of human life, to identify disorders and to find the means to fix them.

The first part of the chapter investigates the *yin* and *yang*, in nature and in human beings, and introduces some series of five.

The second part explains the great correlations between the

five *zang* organs and the five elements.

The chapter continues with patterns of pathology of excess *yin* or *yang*, making more correlations and models of imbalance in nature and in human beings, and concludes with some general principles for treatment which are the consequence of the knowledge acquired.

Nonetheless, the text is careful not to present nature and human beings simply as a mechanical play of *qi*. If the incessant round of change and transformation is well organized by five within the *yin yang* rhythm, then the understanding of the laws ruling the relations and the cycles is rooted and finalized in a vision which goes beyond them.

Certainly, all that is manifest can be studied, known and understood by these means, offering a good basis for efficient action. But that which allows all these manifestations, that which is at the source of every life, belongs to the heavenly mystery – of which the spirits are emissaries. Only that which which is beyond all manifestation can give life and knowledge their unity and their meaning.

Suwen chapter 5 echoes numerous other texts written between the 4th and 1st centuries BCE. Below are some examples from the Great Commentary of the Book of Change or Xici :

'*Yin* then *yang* – that is called the *dao* (the way that life proceeds).'

'To understand change is called "the way things have to be done".'

'That which cannot be penetrated by (means of) *yin yang* is called the spirits.'

'He who knows change and transformation knows what is achieved by the spirits.'

Elisabeth Rochat de la Vallée, Paris 2011

NEIJING SUWEN CHAPTER 5

THE TEXT

黃帝曰
陰陽者天地之道也
萬物之綱紀
變化之父母
生殺之本始
神明之府也
治病必求於本

故積陽為天
積陰為地
陰靜陽躁
陽生陰長
陽殺陰藏
陽化氣陰成形

寒極生熱
熱極生寒
寒氣生濁
熱氣生清

The Yellow Emperor said:
Yinyang is the way of heaven and earth,
The laws and principles of the ten thousand beings,
Father and mother of change and transformation,
Root and beginning of life and death,
Dwelling place of the radiance of the spirits. (2)

To treat disease one has to go to the root. (3)

Therefore, *yang*, accumulated, forms heaven,
Yin, accumulated, forms earth. (4)
Yin is stillness, *yang* is movement;
Yang brings into being, *yin* leads to growth;
Yang puts to death, *yin* buries. (5)
Yang transforms the *qi*, *yin* completes the form. (6)

Extreme cold gives rise to heat;
Extreme heat gives rise to cold. (7)
Cold *qi* generate the turbid;
Hot *qi* generate the clear. (8)

清氣在下則生飧泄
濁氣在上則生䐜脹

此陰陽反作病之逆從也

故
清陽為天
濁陰為地
地氣上為雲
天氣下為雨
雨出地氣
雲出天氣

故
清陽出上竅
濁陰出下竅
清陽發腠理
濁陰走五藏
清陽實四支
濁陰歸六府

When below, the clear *qi* produce diarrhoea containing undigested food;
When above, the turbid *qi* produce distension and swelling. (9)

Disease arises from the contrary actions of *yinyang*, for these run counter to the natural order of life. (10)

Thus, clear *yang* forms heaven,
Turbid *yin* forms earth;
Ascending, earth *qi* forms clouds,
Descending, heavenly *qi* forms rain;
Rain comes from earth *qi*,
Clouds come from heavenly *qi*. (11)

Similarly, clear *yang* appears at the upper orifices,
While turbid *yin* appears at the lower orifices.
Clear *yang* spreads up to the texture of the skin,
While turbid *yin* goes to the five *zang*.
Clear *yang* gives fullness to the four limbs,
While turbid *yin* belongs to the six *fu*. (12)

16 • SUWEN CHAPTER 5

水為陰　火為陽
陽為氣　陰為味

味歸形　形歸氣　氣歸精　精歸化

精食氣　形食味　化生精　氣生形

味傷形　氣傷精　精化為氣　氣傷於味

陰味出下竅　陽氣出上竅

Water is *yin*, fire is *yang*.
Yang makes the *qi*, *yin* makes the tastes. (13)

The tastes belong to the form,
The form belongs to the *qi*,
The *qi* belong to the essences,
The essences belong to transformation. (14)

The essences are nourished by the *qi*,
The body is nourished by the tastes;
Transformation produces the essences,
The *qi* produce the body. (15)

The tastes injure the body,
The *qi* injure the essences;
The essences, through transformations, make the *qi*,
The *qi* are injured by the tastes. (16)

Being *yin*, the tastes are released at the lower orifices;
Being *yang*, the *qi* are released at the upper orifices. (17)

味厚者為陰
薄為陰之陽
氣厚者為陽
薄為陽之陰
味厚則泄
薄則通
氣薄則發泄
厚則發熱

壯火之氣衰
少火之氣壯
壯火食氣
氣食少火
壯火散氣
少火生氣

味辛甘發散為陽
氣酸苦涌泄為陰

When dense, the tastes are *yin*,
When dilute, they are *yang* in the *yin*;
When dense, the *qi* are *yang*,
When dilute, they are *yin* in the *yang*. (18)
When dense, the tastes stimulate evacuation,
When dilute, they stimulate circulation;
When dilute, the *qi* cause outbreaks of sweating,
When dense, they cause outbreaks of heat. (19)

A strong fire decreases the *qi*,
A gentle fire strengthens the *qi*;
A strong fire feeds on the *qi*,
The *qi* feed on a gentle fire;
A strong fire dispels the *qi*,
A gentle fire produces the *qi*. (20)

As to *qi* and tastes,
Pungent and sweet, which cause things to burst forth and spread out, are *yang*;
Sour and bitter, which cause things to rise up and be eliminated, are *yin*. (21)

陰勝則陽病
陽勝則陰病
陽勝則熱
陰勝則寒
重寒則熱
重熱則寒

寒傷形
熱傷氣
氣傷痛
形傷腫

故先痛而後腫者氣傷形也
先腫而後痛者形傷氣也

風勝則動
熱勝則腫
燥勝則乾
寒勝則浮
濕勝則濡瀉

When *yin* prevails, *yang* is diseased,
When *yang* prevails, *yin* is diseased; (22)
When *yang* prevails, there is heat,
When *yin* prevails, there is cold; (23)
Increasing cold results in heat;
Increasing heat results in cold. (24)

Cold injures the form,
Heat injures the *qi*. (25)
Injury to the *qi* gives rise to pain,
Injury to the form gives rise to swelling. (26)

Therefore, if there is first pain then swelling,
The *qi* are injuring the form;
And if there is first swelling and then pain,
The form is injuring the *qi*. (27)

If wind prevails, there is agitation;
If heat prevails, there is swelling;
If dryness prevails, there is drying out;
If cold prevails, there is bloating;
If dampness prevails, there is liquid diarrhoea. (28)

天有四時五行
以生長收藏
以生寒暑燥濕風
人有五藏化五氣
以生喜怒悲憂恐

故
喜怒傷氣
寒暑傷形
暴怒傷陰
暴喜傷陽
厥氣上行
滿脈去形
喜怒不節
寒暑過度
生乃不固

故重陰必陽
重陽必陰

Heaven has four seasons and five elements (29)
For generating, growing, gathering and burying, (30)
And to produce cold, heat, dryness, dampness and wind. (31)
Human beings have five *zang* and,
through transformation, five *qi*, (32)
Which produce elation, anger, sadness, oppressive grief and fear. (33)

Thus elation and anger injure the *qi*,
Cold and heat injure the form. (34)
Violent anger injures the *yin*, (35)
Violent elation injures the *yang*. (36)
When *qi* rise up in reverse,
They congest the vital circulation and leave the body. (37)
If elation and anger are not well regulated,
If cold and heat are excessive,
Life is no longer secure. (38)

So increasing *yin* turns into *yang*
And increasing *yang* turns into *yin*. (39)

故曰

冬傷於寒春必溫病
春傷於風夏生飧泄
夏傷於暑秋必痎瘧
秋傷於濕冬生咳嗽

Therefore it is said:

Injury by cold in winter leads to warm diseases in spring (40)
Injury by wind in spring leads to diarrhoea with undigested food in summer. (41)
Injury by heat in summer leads to intermittent fevers in autumn. (42)
Injury by dampness in autumn leads to coughing in winter. (43)

帝曰余聞

上古聖人論理人形
列別藏府端絡經脈
會通六合各從其經
氣穴所發各有處名
谿谷屬骨皆有所起
分部逆從各有經理
四時陰陽盡有經紀
外內之應皆有表裡
其信然乎

The Emperor said:
I was taught
That the sages of ancient time presented the principles organising the human body,
Ordering and differentiating the *zang* and the *fu*,
determining the extremities and branchings of the meridians, (44)
Grouping them together to ensure free communication in the six junctions, each according to its proper norms; (45)
Assigning to each cavity of *qi* that springs forth a location and name; (46)
Recognising how activity arises from the ravines and the valleys, and the bones which support them; (47)
Giving to each well-divided region, with its currents and counter-currents, the principle of organisation; (48)
Giving the *yinyang* of the four seasons the cycles of its regular course; (49)
Recognising all the outward and inward exchanges in the correspondences between the exterior and the interior. (50)

Are we really to put our faith in that?

岐伯對曰

東方生風
風生木
木生酸
酸生肝
肝生筋
筋生心
肝主目

其在天為玄
在人為道
在地化生五味
道生智
玄生神

神在天為風
在地為木
在體為筋
在藏為肝
在色為蒼

Qi Bo replied: (51)
The eastern quarter produces wind, (51)
Wind produces wood, (53)
Wood produces the sour, (54)
Sour produces the liver, (55)
The liver produces muscular movement, (56)
Muscular movement produces the heart; (57)
The liver masters the eyes. (58)

In heaven, it is the deep mystery,
In man, it is the *dao*,
On earth, it is transformation.
Transformation produces the five tastes,
The *dao* produces wisdom,
The deep mystery produces the spirits. (59)

The spirits!
In heaven are wind,
On earth are wood,
Of the parts of the body are muscular movement,
Of *zang*, the liver,
Of colour, green-blue, (60)

在音為角
在聲為呼
在變動為握
在竅為目
在味為酸
在志為怒

怒傷肝
悲勝怒
風傷筋
燥勝風
酸傷筋
辛勝酸

Of musical tones, it is *jue*, (61)
Of sounds, it is shouting, (62)
Of reactions to change, it is contraction, (63)
Of orifices, it is the eyes,
Of tastes, it is sour,
Of expressions of will, it is anger. (64)

Anger injures the liver, sadness prevails over anger; (65)
Wind injures muscular movement, dryness prevails over wind; (66)
Sour injures muscular movement, bitter prevails over sour. (67)

南方生熱
熱生火
火生苦
苦生心
心生血
血生脾
心主舌

其在天為熱
在地為火
在體為脈
在藏為心
在色為赤
在音為徵
在聲為笑
在變動為笑
在竅為舌
在味為苦
在志為喜
憂

喜傷心
恐勝喜
熱傷氣
寒勝熱
苦傷氣
鹹勝苦

The southern quarter produces heat, (68)

Heat produces fire, (69)

Fire produces the bitter, (70)

Bitter produces the heart, (71)

The heart produces blood, (72)

Blood produces the spleen; (73)

The heart masters the tongue. (74)

In heaven it is heat,

On earth it is fire,

Of the parts of the body, it is the vital circulation, (75)

Of the *zang* organs, it is the heart,

Of colours, it is red, (76)

Of musical tones, it is *zhi* (77)

Of sounds, it is laughter, (78)

Of reactions to change, it is oppressive grief, (79)

Of orifices, it is the tongue,

Of tastes, it is bitter,

Of expressions of will, it is elation. (80)

Elation injures the heart, fear prevails over elation. (81)

Heat injures the *qi*, cold prevails over heat. (82)

Bitter injures the *qi*, salty prevails over bitter. (83)

中央生濕
濕生土
土生甘
甘生脾
脾生肉
肉生肺
脾主口

其在天為濕
在地為土
在體為肉
在藏為脾
在色為黃
在音為宮
在聲為歌
在變動為噦
在竅為口
在味為甘
在志為思

思傷脾
怒勝思
濕傷肉
風勝濕
甘傷肉
酸勝甘

The central region produces dampness, (84)
Dampness produces earth, (85)
Earth produces the sweet, (86)
Sweet produces the spleen, (87)
The spleen produces the flesh, (88)
The flesh produces the lung; (89)
The spleen masters the mouth. (90)

In heaven, it is dampness,
On earth, it is the earth,
Of the parts of the body, it is flesh,
Of the *zang* organs, it is the spleen,
Of colours, it is yellow, (91)
Of musical tones, it is *gong*, (92)
Of sounds, it is singing, (93)
Of reactions to change, it is belching, (94)
Of orifices, it is the mouth,
Of tastes, it is sweet,
Of expressions of will, it is thought. (95)

Obsessive thought injures the spleen, anger prevails over obsessive thought. (96)
Dampness injures the flesh, wind prevails over dampness. (97)
Sweet injures the flesh, sour prevails over sweet. (98)

西方生燥
燥生金
金生辛
辛生肺
肺生皮毛
皮毛生腎
肺主鼻

其在天為燥
在地為金
在體為皮毛
在藏為肺
在色為白
在音為商
在聲為哭
在變動為咳
在竅為鼻
在味為辛
在志為憂

憂傷肺
喜勝憂
熱傷皮毛
寒勝熱
辛傷皮毛
苦勝辛

The western quarter produces dryness, (99)
Dryness produces metal, (100)
Metal produces the pungent, (101)
Pungent produces the lung, (102)
The lung produces skin and body hair, (103)
Skin and body hair produce the kidneys; (104)
The lung masters the nose. (105)

In heaven, it is dryness,
On earth, it is metal,
Of the parts of the body, it is the skin and body hair,
Of the *zang* organs, it is the lung,
Of colour, it is white, (106)
Of musical tones, it is *shang*, (107)
Of sounds, it is sobbing, (108)
Of reactions to change, it is coughing, (109)
Of orifices, it is the nose,
Of tastes, it is pungent,
Of expressions of will, it is oppressive grief. (110)

Oppressive grief injures the lung, elation prevails over oppressive grief. (111) Heat injures the skin and body hair, cold prevails over heat. (112) Pungent injures the skin and body hair, bitter prevails over pungent. (113)

北方
生寒
寒生水
水生鹹
鹹生腎
腎生骨髓
髓生肝
腎主耳

其在天為寒
在地為水
在體為骨
在藏為腎
在色為黑
在音為羽
在聲為呻
在變動為慄
在竅為耳
在味為鹹
在志為恐

恐傷腎
思勝恐
寒傷血
燥勝寒
鹹傷血
甘勝鹹

The northern region produces cold, (114)
Cold produces water, (115)
Water produces the salty, (116)
Salty produces the kidneys, (117)
The kidneys produce bone and marrow, (118)
Marrow produces the liver; (119)
The kidneys master the ears. (120)

In heaven, it is cold,
On earth, it is water,
Of the parts of the body, it is bone,
Of the *zang* organs it is the kidneys,
Of colours, it is black, (121)
Of musical tones, it is *yu*, (122)
Of sounds, it is sighing, (123)
Of reactions to change, it is shivering, (124)
Of orifices, it is the ears,
Of tastes, it is salty,
Of expressions of will, it is fear. (125)

Fear injures the kidneys, thought prevails over fear. (126)
Cold injures the blood, dryness prevails over cold. (127)
Salty injures the blood, sweet prevails over salty. (128)

故曰
天地者萬物之上下也
陰陽者血氣之男女也
左右者陰陽之道路也
水火者陰陽之徵兆也
陰陽者萬物之能始也

故曰
陰在內陽之守也
陽在外陰之使也

帝曰
法陰陽奈何

岐伯曰
陽勝則身熱腠理閉喘粗為之俛仰
汗不出而熱齒乾以煩冤腹滿死
能冬不能夏

Thus it is said:
Heaven and earth are the high and the low for the ten thousand beings (129)
And *yinyang* the male and female for blood and *qi* (130)
Left and right the paths and routes for *yinyang* (131)
Water and fire the expression and revelation of *yinyang* (132)
Yinyang is the power and the beginning of the ten thousand beings. (133)

So it is said:
Yin is on the inside but *yang* keeps it there;
Yang is on the outside but *yin* sends it there. (134)

The Emperor asked:
What is the norm in terms of *yinyang*? (135)

Qi Bo replied:
When *yang* prevails, (136) the body heats up and the pores of the skin close, (137) noisy and laboured breathing causes the head to droop and lift, (138) sweat cannot escape and heat becomes intense, (139) the teeth dry out, (140) one suffers from burning disease, (141) the abdomen is congested and death ensues. (142) It is possible to survive in winter, but not in summer. (143)

陰勝則身寒汗出身常清數慄而寒
寒則厥厥則腹滿死能夏不能冬
此陰陽更勝之變病之形能也

帝曰
調此二者奈何

岐伯曰
能知七損八益則二者可調
不知用此則早衰之節也

年四十而陰氣自半也起居衰矣
年五十體重耳目不聰明矣
年六十陰痿氣大衰九竅不利
下虛上實涕泣俱出矣

When *yin* prevails, the body becomes cold and sweats, (144) the body is permanently frozen, (145) shaken by shivering, the cold intensifies; (146) the cold causes weakening, (147) the abdomen becomes congested; death ensues.(148) It is possible to survive in summer, but not in winter.

These are the changes according to the contrasting prevalence of *yin* and *yang* revealing the manifestation and virulence of diseases.

The Emperor asked:
How are these two set right?

Qi Bo replied:
If one knows the seven decreasings and the eight increasings, (149) one is able to regulate both; (150) but acting without this knowledge one declines prematurely. (151)

At forty, *yin qi* are reduced by half, activity declines; (152) At fifty, the body is heavy, the ears and eyes have lost their quickness and sharpness; (153) At sixty, the *yin* is impotent, the *qi* decline greatly, the nine orifices lose their ease of function, there is emptiness below and fullness above, nasal mucus and tears flow out. (154)

故曰
知之則強不知則老

故同出而名異耳

智者察同愚者察異

愚者不足智者有餘

有餘則耳目聰明身體輕強

老者復壯壯者益治

是以聖人為無為之事
樂恬憺之能
從欲快志於虛無之守
故壽命無窮
與天地終
此聖人之治身也

Thus it is said:
The strength of those who know will be maintained;
ageing will occur in those who do not know. (155)
Thus, 'Coming from the same origin, they will
nonetheless be given different names.' (155)
Where those who have true knowledge see sameness,
those who do not know see difference. (157)
Those who do not know always lack something,
While those who know have in abundance, (158)
An abundance which appears as sharpness and quickness
of ears and eyes, and an alert and robust body.
Even when old, their vigour returns to them, a vigour
which enables them to conduct their life perfectly. (159)

This is why the sages practised doing by non-doing,
Delighting in their capacity for quiet and serenity,
They followed their desires and benefited from their will,
Remaining within emptiness and nothingness.
Therefore, long life enabled them to accomplish their
destiny, without limitation,
Sharing with heaven and earth until the end.
This is how the sages conducted their lives. (160)

天不足西北
故西北方陰也
而人右耳目不如左明也
地不滿東南方陽也
故東南方陽也
而人左手足不如右強也
帝曰
何以然
岐伯曰
東方陽也陽者其精并於上并於上則上明而下虛
故使耳目聰明而手足不便也
西方陰也陰者其精并於下并於下則下盛而上虛
故其耳目不聰明而手足便也

Heaven is deficient in the north-west,
Therefore the western and northern quarters are *yin*,
And in man ear and eye are not as clear on the right as on the left.
Earth is not full in the south-east,
Therefore the eastern and southern quarters are *yang*,
And in man hand and foot are not as strong on the left as on the right. (161)

The Emperor asked:
How is this?

Qi Bo replied:
The eastern quarter is *yang*; with *yang* the essences accumulate above; by accumulating above, what is above is resplendent and what is below becomes empty. This gives sharpness and quickness to ear and eye, while hand and foot do not function as they should. (162)
The western quarter is *yin*, with *yin* the essences accumulate below; by accumulating below, what is below flourishes and what is above becomes empty. Therefore, ear and eye have neither sharpness nor quickness, while hand and foot function as they should. (163)

故俱感於邪其在上則右甚在下則左甚
此天地陰陽所不能全也故邪居之

故天有精地有形
天有八紀地有五理故能為萬物之父母
清陽上天濁陰歸地
是故天地之動靜
神明為之綱紀
故能以生長收藏終而復始

惟賢人
上配天以養頭
下象地以養足
中傍人事以養五藏

Thus, where there is a reaction to the perverse, above the right side is the most affected, but below the left side is the most affected. (164) Because the *yinyang* of heaven and earth itself cannot be whole, the perverse find a place to settle (165)

Thus heaven through its essences and earth through its forms, (166) heaven through the eight regulators and earth through the five organizers, (167) can act as father and mother to the ten thousand beings. (168) Since clear *yang* rises to heaven and turbid *yin* returns to earth, heaven and earth move and are still, the radiance of the spirits forms the net of laws and principles. (169)
Thus, through a process of generating, growing, gathering and burying, everything reaches its term and starts again. (170)

Only the wise,
Above, make themselves companions of heaven to maintain the life of the head; (171)
Below, make themselves into the image of earth to maintain the life of the feet; (172)
In the middle, occupy themselves with human affairs to maintain the life of the five *zang*. (173)

天氣通於肺
地氣通於嗌
風氣通於肝
雷氣通於心
谷氣通於脾
雨氣通於腎
六經為川
腸胃為海
九竅為水注之氣

以天地為之陰陽
陽之汗以天地之雨名之
陽之氣以天地之疾風名之
暴氣象雷
逆氣象陽
故治不法天之紀不用地之理則災害至矣
故邪風之至疾如風雨

The *qi* of heaven commune with the lungs, (174)
The *qi* of earth commune with the throat, (175)
The *qi* of wind commune with the liver, (176)
The *qi* of thunder commune with the heart, (177)
The *qi* of the valleys commune with the spleen, (178)
The *qi* of rain commune with the kidneys. (179)
The six meridians are like rivers, (180)
The intestines and stomach are like seas, (181)
The nine orifices are like *qi* pouring forth as water. (182)

In considering *yinyang* in its relation to heaven and earth,
Sweat is called *yang*, taking its name from the rain of heaven and earth. (183)
Qi is called *yang*, taking its name from the rapid wind of heaven and earth. (184)
When *qi* is violent, it takes on the image of thunder, (185)
And when it runs counter to its proper course, it takes on the image of *yang*. (186)

Therefore, to treat without the regulators of heaven as model and ignoring the organiszers of earth, leads to disaster and catastrophe. (187) Perverse winds occur with the violence of a storm. (188)

故善治者治皮毛其次治肌膚其次治筋脈其次治六府其次治五藏治五藏者半死半生也

故天之邪氣感則害人五藏
水穀之寒熱感則害於六府
地之濕氣感則害皮肉筋脈

故善用鍼者 從陰引陽 從陽引陰 以右治左 以左治右 以我知彼 以表知裡 以觀過與不及之理 見微得過 用之不殆

Thus he who excels in the art of healing will first treat the skin and body hair, then treat at the surface of the flesh, then treat the muscular movement and vital circulation, then treat the six *fu*, then treat the five *zang*; in treating the five *zang*, half will die and half will live. (189)

Thus when the perverse *qi* of heaven affect man, they harm his five *zang* (190): when heat and cold, due to liquid and solid food, affect man, they harm his six *fu* (191): and when the damp *qi* of earth affect man, they harm his skin, flesh, muscular movement and vital circulation. (192)

Thus he who excels with needles draws *yang* from *yin* and *yin* from *yang*. (193) He treats the left side on the right and the right side on the left. (194) Through what is his he reaches the other. (195) Through the manifest he reaches the inner organization. (196) Merely by observing what causes excess and what is deficient, he perceives what is most subtle and reveals what is not right. (197)
His art is always faultless. (198)

善診者
察色按脈先別陰陽
審清濁而知部分
視喘息聽音聲而知所苦
觀權衡規矩而知病所主
按尺寸觀浮沈滑濇而知病所生以治
無過以診則不失矣

故曰
病之始起也可刺而已
其盛可待衰而已

故因其輕而揚之
因其重而減之
因其衰而彰之

He who excels in diagnosis examines the complexion
and takes the pulse, above all to assess *yin* and *yang*. (199)
He locates where there is a problem by assessing what is
clear and what is turbid. (200) He perceives where there is
disease by assessing difficulties in breathing and listening
to sounds and noises.(201) He perceives what is controlling
the disease by observing the power and the balance of the
round and the square. (202) He perceives what has caused
the disease by taking the pulse on the proximal and distal
positions, and by observing whether they are superficial or
deep, slippery or choppy. (203)
His treatment is then faultless, because his diagnosis never
errs. (204)

Thus it is said:
When illness first appears,
We need only needle, and it is gone.
If it has developed further,
We must wait until it decreases and then it will cease. (205)

So, faced with a benign situation, drain;
Faced with a serious situation, reduce;
Faced with a situation in decline, restore resplendence. (206)

形不足者溫之以氣
精不足者補之以味

其高者因而越之
其下者引而竭之
中滿者瀉之於內

其有邪者漬形以為汗
其在皮者汗而發之
其慓悍者按而收之
其實者散而瀉之

審其陰陽以別柔剛
陽病治陰陰病治陽
定其血氣各守其鄉
血實宜決之
氣虛宜掣引之

If the deficiency is in the body, warm by the *qi*. (207)
If the deficiency is in the essences, tonify by the tastes. (208)

If the upper areas are affected, expel towards the outside. (209)
If the lower areas are affected, drain to empty them. (210)
If the centre is congested, disperse internally. (211)

In case of perverse *qi*, flush the body by profuse sweating. (212)
If at the level of the skin, induce an outbreak of sweat. (213)
If lively and active, compress and gather in. (214)
If full, spread and disperse. (215)

Yin and *yang* are examined to differentiate between the soft and the hard. (216)
In *yang* disease treat by the *yin*, and in *yin* disease treat by the *yang*,
Stabilize blood and *qi* and ensure that each remains within its own territory. (217)
If there is an excess of blood, a way must be cleared,
And if there is emptiness of *qi*, they must be drawn in and guided. (218)

NEIJING SUWEN CHAPTER 5

TEXTUAL NOTES

1. 陰陽應象大論篇第五
yin yang ying xiang da lun pian di wu

Chapter Five: The great treatise on the correspondance of phenomena to *yinyang* (title to chapter)

Yinyang, the alternating rhythm at the heart of the world, constitutes all that exists, all the phenomena that are. *Yinyang* is a tool to analyze, qualify and understand reality; but reality itself is beyond any analysis, qualification or intellectual interpretation. Nevertheless, interpretation of reality by means of *yinyang* is solid and reliable. It gives us a basis on which to act, and within this specific context, a way to diagnose and treat.

2. 黃帝曰陰陽者天地之道也萬物之綱紀
Huang di yue yin yang zhe tian di zhi dao ye wan wu zhi gang ji
變化之父母生殺之本始神明之府也
Bian hua zhi fu mu sheng sha zhi ben shi shen ming zhi fu ye

The Yellow Emperor said: *yinyang* is the way of heaven and earth, the laws and principles of the ten thousand beings, father and mother of change and transformation, root and beginning of life and death, dwelling place of the radiance of the spirits.

This is a five-fold exposition of the aspects through which *yinyang* manifests itself to us. The couples are modelled upon *yinyang*, thus gradually creating the mesh of life.

This is the way of heaven and earth: human beings live, mysteriously, in the embrace of heaven, which gives rise to their appearance and constantly draws them back, and of earth, which forms them and constantly supports them. *Yinyang* is a way, a means, by which heaven and earth express their creative power.

Great laws and principles are expressed by the image of a master rope and its meshes: the *yang* and the *qi* ensure the norms and maintain their uprightness and unity. The *yin*, which nourishes and supports the multiplicity of manifestations, knits together all the individual structures whose task it is to receive life. All beings are caught in the net of *yinyang*. The hard and the soft are good examples of the structure which holds and forms all beings. The image given is of a strong rope which acts as support, and the many meshes which knit it all together and contain it. *Yin* and *yang* are flesh and bone for all forms.

'Father and mother of change and transformation': the different compositions of *yin* and *yang* create all variety of species and all possibile appearances within human beings. They also ensure the development of each individual as they constantly transform themselves.

'Root and beginning of life and death': at the beginning of the world, of a species, of a being, of a season, etc., there is a specific quality of *qi*, defined by its *yinyang* composition. This composition contains within it the conditions for its development and the limits placed upon it. The natural ending of our being is present in our beginning. All cycles can be expressed in terms of *yinyang*, and all life evolves according to these cycles.

'Dwelling place of the radiance of the spirits' (*shen ming* 神 明): the play of *yinyang* ceaselessly knits together all the manifestations of life, which appear in our bodies through the bloom of our flesh, the brightness of our eyes and the lush redness of our lips. But it is the spirits which direct life and guide the exchanges and reciprocal action of *yinyang*, so that all that creates a living being is not simply the result of a *yinyang* mechanism but an expression of the power which lies beyond *yin* and *yang* and whose presence is revealed through *yinyang*, that of the spirits flourishing in their serenity. *Yinyang* acts as a reservoir for the manifestation of the spirits, which can thus reveal the splendour of what exists. The spirits exist as a result of the harmonious balance of *yinyang*, since this is the perfect functioning and natural order of life.

The blood-*qi* relationship which, in a human being, expresses the harmony of *yinyang*, is magnified between the heart, master of the blood, and the lung, master of the *qi*, in the Sea of *Qi* at the centre of the chest, where all *yin qi* and *yang qi* merge. Blood-and-*qi* distribute the power of the spirits and ensure the strength of the body, the colour of the skin, the regular beat of the pulse, and so on.

3. 治病必求於本
zhi bing bi qiu yu ben
To treat disease one has to go to the root.

It is not enough merely to suppress a symptom; the vital movement has to be re-established where it has become disturbed, at its source, and thus at the root where life begins its series of heavenly changes and earthly transformations. This will enable us to perceive the pattern to which each corresponds.

To return to the root means to return to the patient's *yinyang*, and through this to the spirits where all deviations from the natural movement originate (cf. Lingshu chapter 8).

4 故積陽為天積陰為地
gu ji yang wei tian ji yin wei di
Therefore *yang*, accumulated, forms heaven, *yin*, accumulated, forms earth.

Heaven and earth are formed from the most extreme expressions of the qualities of *yang* and *yin* respectively:

> 'That which is pure and bright spreads out to form heaven;
> The heavy and turbid congeals to form earth.'
> (Huainanzi ch.3, trans Major)

To accumulate (*ji* 積), rather than to build up, indicates that the same movement is repeated, gradually adding strength to a specific virtue or power. The constant extraction of what is pure and subtle forms heaven, and gives heaven its quality of being heaven, of expressing at its most extreme the quality specific to the *yang*. The same is true, in its own way, of the earth.

5. 陰靜陽躁陽生陰長陽殺陰藏
yin jing yang zao, yang sheng yin zhang yang sha yin cang

Yin is stillness, *yang* is movement; *yang* brings into being, *yin* leads to growth; *yang* puts to death, *yin* buries.

Within the *yang* seasons there is a *yang* aspect which is the upsurge (spring) and a *yin* aspect which is its maturing, its fulfilment (summer).

Within the *yin* seasons, there is a *yang* aspect which reflects a reversal (autumn) and a *yin* aspect which reflects the disappearance, the submerging, of the traces of life (winter). *Yang* starts the movement, reflecting that of heaven, and provides the impetus, while *yin* follows, gives form and completes, in the manner of earth.

6. 陽 化 氣 陰 成 形
   yang hua qi yin cheng xing
   Yang transforms the *qi*, *yin* completes the form.

The *yang*, which represents movement and diffusion, initiates every process and gives power to its transformations. The *yin*, which represents repose and condensation, gathers in, nourishes, shapes and forms.

7. 寒 極 生 熱 熱 極 生 寒
   han ji sheng re, re ji sheng han
   Extreme cold gives rise to heat; extreme heat gives rise to cold.

Life oscillates between the exchanges of *yinyang*, one of whose manifestations is cold and heat. The seasons are visible expressions of these successive states; the end of winter, for example, is followed by the start of spring. But they also teach us about what takes place in secret within the seasons. Summer comes into being in the heart of winter, just as it is at noon that the day starts to decline. There is a constant rhythm of alternation and reversal. In pathology, it should therefore not surprise us to find that a sudden cold can quickly turn into a fever, or a strong fever leave us weak and cold.

8. 寒氣生濁熱氣生清
han qi sheng zhuo re qi sheng qing
Cold *qi* generate the turbid; hot *qi* generate the clear.

The turbid (*zhuo* 濁) describes that which descends and becomes concentrated, as in the formation of the earth. The cold, as an expression of *yin*, intensifies this movement. The clear (*qing* 清) describes that which rises and disseminates, as in the formation of heaven. The hot, as an expression of *yang*, stimulates this movement.

In physiology, two typical examples might be the fire of *mingmen*, which produces heat and causes the clear to rise in the body, and the freshness of the lung, leading to condensation of the turbid, which then descends to the base of the trunk.

9. 清氣在下則生飧泄濁氣在上則生䐜脹
Qing qi zai xia ze sheng sun xie zhuo qi zai shang ze sheng chen zhang
When below, the clear *qi* produce diarrhoea containing undigested food; when above, the turbid *qi* produce distension and swelling.

If what is 'clear', and therefore rich in essences, is found in the lower part of the body, it indicates that 'the clear' has not been assimilated and directed properly.

Conversely, if 'the turbid', that which is weighed down with what cannot be incorporated within the organism, is in the upper part of the body (which houses the subtle aspects of life, and where the spirits gain support from the purest of essences), it will cause the tissues to become heavy and impregnated, and there will be a corresponding increase in volume.

Thus, if the fire of *mingmen* decreases, weakening the digestive capacity of the spleen and the stomach, substance will not be retained and assimilation will be incomplete, leading to diarrhoea containing undigested food.

If the lung no longer causes the turbid to descend, the lung itself, and the whole area lying above the diaphragm, will lose its clarity and purity, leading to all kinds of congestive problems.

10. 此陰陽反作病之逆從也
   ci yin yang fan zuo bing zhi ni cong ye

Disease arises from the contrary actions of *yinyang*, for these run counter to the natural order of life.

The perfect interplay of *yinyang* in time and space represents the natural order, which forms the very movement of life. Any malfunctioning of the normal and complementary exchanges of *yinyang* lies at the origin of all disease. This becomes increasingly serious, since the movement running counter to the proper flow has a tendency to replace the natural movement at an ever deeper level.

11. 故清陽為天濁陰為地地氣上為雲天氣下為雨
    gu qing yang wei tian zhuo yin wei di di qi shang wei yun tian qi xia wei yu
    雨出地氣雲出天氣
    yu chu di qi yun chu tian qi

Thus, clear *yang* forms heaven, turbid *yin* forms earth; ascending, earth *qi* forms clouds, descending, heavenly *qi* forms rain; rain comes from earth *qi*, clouds come from heavenly *qi*.

Clouds are formed by the evaporation of the humidity of the earth by the heat of the sun. They come both from heaven and from earth, because they need both the contribution of earth, in terms of their substance, and the warmth of the *yang* as well as the movements of *qi* in heaven.

Rain, too, which is the result of condensation, by cooling, in heaven, is caused by humidity rising from the earth. In heaven, clouds indicate the presence of humidity rising from the earth. They owe their subtlety and movement to the *yang* of heaven, but their presence shows that the earth has sufficient subtlety and clarity to offer to heaven. Rain is the manifestation of condensation and cooling taking place in the sky above, revealing a *yin* movement in heaven and showing that there is *yin* in heaven.

It is easy to see in this an analogy with the fire of *mingmen* and with the lung's function of cooling and clarifying through its downward movement (*qing su* 清肅).

12. 故 清 陽 出 上 竅 濁 陰 出 下 竅 清 陽 發 腠 理
gu qing yang chu shang qiao zhuo yin chu xia qiao qing yang fa cou li
濁 陰 走 五 藏 清 陽 實 四 支 濁 陰 歸 六 府
zhuo yin zou wu zang qing yang shi si zhi zhuo yin gui liu fu

Similarly, clear *yang* appears at the upper orifices, while turbid *yin* appears at the lower orifices. Clear *yang* spreads up to the texture of the skin, while turbid *yin* goes to the five *zang*. Clear *yang* gives fullness to the four limbs, while turbid *yin* belongs to the six *fu*.

Since the only true definition of what is clear is a movement which rises up and diffuses, and of what is turbid is a movement which moves things down and condenses, we can understand how clear *yang* and turbid *yin* can modulate what they represent in the body and, through their relationship to each other, reverse the order or priority of vital energy.

The upper orifices represent the upper part of the body, where the subtlety of essences and the purity of *qi* reach their maximum height and diffusion; the clear *yang* can then help the brain and the sense organs to function with power and subtlety.

Turbid *yin* represents the opposite of this; it is what remains after the assimilation, release and movement upwards of what is 'clear' in food. It represents the concentration of the chyle and the descent of waste and dregs as they are evacuated by the lower orifices of the body.

The texture of the skin (*cou li* 腠 理) represents the final stage in the diffusion of *yang* as it rises up towards the external areas of the body. Sweat is one manifestation of this, and our defensive *qi* (*wei qi*) another. This is the centrifugal movement of vital energy.

The five *zang* fill themselves with essences, with turbid *yin*, that is with vital energy which has a centripetal movement. Here turbid *yin* refers to the essences; it is more subtle than clear *yang* and forms the basis for its power.

The four limbs are the external, visible, controlled movements where vital energy expresses itself. The six *fu* form the internal, invisible and instinctive transformations through which the vital energy recharges itself from the very substance of food.

13. 水為陰火為陽 陽為氣陰為味
shui wei yin huo wei yang yang wei qi yin wei wei
Water is *yin* and fire is *yang*. *Yang* makes the *qi*, and *yin* makes the tastes.

Yinyang is presented here in the form of the first traces perceptible on earth, which are water and fire, mixing together to create all life. According to the Hongfan, they are the first two elements to appear, and form the basis of any manifestation of life. They constitute the great vertical axis of the rooting of an individual destiny.

Experience has shown us the effects of water and fire. By analogy, the *qi* and the tastes are presented as being the two great *yin* and *yang* principles involved in the renewal and control of life. Here *qi* and tastes are seen as all that is incorporated in a human being to enable it to reconstitute itself. *Qi* and tastes mix with each other as do water and fire, modelling themselves upon *yinyang*.

14. 味歸形 形歸氣 氣歸精 精歸化
wei gui xing xing gui qi   qi gui jing   jing gui hua
The tastes belong to the form, the form belongs to the *qi*, the *qi* belong to the essences, the essences belong to transformation.

Five concepts are presented here: tastes, body, *qi*, essences and transformations, in a subtle interplay of *yinyang*, where the *qi* take up a pivotal, working position. Their relationship to each of the four other concepts is discussed in the text that follows. Tastes are represented here by the quality they show in renewing vital energy; they can be good or bad, beneficial or harmful. This is what differentiates them from essences, which are always pure, rich, vital, inalterable and faithful to the human being which they make up.

Tastes (*wei* 味) reconstitute the form. The form (*xing* 形) is the place where the *qi* express themselves, it holds them and makes it possible for them to express themselves. The *qi* are the servants of the essences, protecting them and ensuring their permanence. The essences (*jing* 精) are effective only because of the transformations which are carried out by the power of the *qi*, and for which they form the foundation. The transformations (*hua* 化) are the mystery of life on earth.

Here we are penetrating deep within a human being, from the assimilation of what is external (tastes) to the most intimate functions of life (transformation). This helps us to understand why food, diet and remedies are considered so important.

15. 精 食 氣 形 食 味 化 生 精 氣 生 形
jing shi qi xing shi wei hua sheng jing qi sheng xing

The essences are nourished by the *qi*, the body is nourished by the tastes; transformation produces the essences, the *qi* produce the body.

The relationships are discussed in greater detail by reversing the order of the preceding paragraph. The essences make use of the *qi* and of the transformations to enable them to be extracted, refined, assimilated and directed in the desired form, and thus to renew the body, starting from its deepest aspect.

16. 味 傷 形 氣 傷 精 精 化 為 氣 氣 傷 於 味
wei shang xing qi shang jing jing hua wei qi qi shang yu wei

The tastes injure the body, the *qi* injure the essences; the essences, through transformations, make the *qi*, the *qi* are injured by the tastes.

Human beings bring pathology, which interferes with the normal processes of heaven and earth. The same relationships are maintained, but they become disturbed, as the vital energy turns into perverse energy. Excessive tastes attack the body at different levels (this will be shown a little later on in the chapter), as the sour taste causes muscular contractions, for example, (cf. Suwen chapters 9 and 10).

When the *qi* become too weak, they gradually lose their power to renew, transform or protect the essences; on the other hand, when they become too strong, they burn and destroy the *yin*, which forms the fluids secreted by the essences: the *qi* injure the essences.

If the tastes are not sufficient, or of sufficient quality, the *zang* do not receive vital essences and consequently the qi cannot be sustained. Thus the tastes injure the *qi*.

17. 陰 味 出 下 竅 陽 氣 出 上 竅
yin wei chu xia qiao yang qi chu shang qiao
Being *yin*, the tastes are released at the lower orifices; being *yang*, the *qi* are released at the upper orifices.

Yin is the fundamental movement of the earth, which is to condense and descend, and *yang* the formative movement of heaven, which is to expand and ascend. Tastes, being *yin*, reproduce this movement in the body, whilst the *qi* express the movement specific to the *yang*. Concentrated matter is eliminated by the lower orifices, whilst the upper orifices are where clear *yang*, rich in essences, is released, to give life to the brain and the sense organs.

18. 味 厚 者 為 陰 薄 為 陰 之 陽 氣 厚 者 為 陽 薄 為 陽 之 陰
Wei hou zhe wei yin bo wei yin zhi yang qi hou zhe wei yang bo wei yang zhi yin
When dense, the tastes are *yin*, when dilute, they are *yang* in the *yin*; When dense, the *qi* are *yang*, when dilute, they are *yin* in the *yang*.

It is not enough simply to posit the coupling of *yinyang*, we must also discuss the model which underlies it. At the start of the chapter, we saw a model of *yinyang* in the four seasons, showing the *yin* in the *yang* and the *yang* in the *yin* over the passage of time. The same principle and schema are found in the composition of the *qi* and the tastes. *Yinyang* appears in many combinations, the archetype shown here being a simple way of evoking the variation of *yin* and *yang* in tastes and *qi*.

Density is the purest state of *yin*, dilution the purest state of *yang*. But there is always an appreciable amount of the complementary component.

19. 味 厚 則 泄 薄 則 通 氣 薄 則 發 泄 厚 則 發 熱
wei hou ze xie bo ze tong qi bo ze fa xie hou ze fa re
When dense, the tastes stimulate evacuation, when dilute, they stimulate circulation; when dilute, the *qi* cause outbreaks of sweating, when dense, they cause outbreaks of heat.

The effects produced by the different *yinyang* combinations in the mixture of tastes and *qi* are here expressed from a therapeutic point of view:
 - Evacuation (*xie* 泄) is in the nature of purging, large-scale elimination of bulky matter from below.
 - Circulation (*tong* 通) is a form of activation of the processes of elimination which do not reach the stage of large-scale purges.
 - When sweat pours out and is eliminated (*fa xie* 發 泄), this indicates that the fluid is pushed to the outside by the centrifugal movement of the *yang*, leading to cooling and the elimination of perverse energies.
 - When heat pours out (*fa re* 發 熱), this is the result of a pure form of warming up, created by the stimulation of the *yang* movement and of the *qi*, and resulting in fever or heat.

20. 壯 火 之 氣 衰 少 火 之 氣 壯 壯 火 食 氣
zhuang huo zhi qi shuai shao huo zhi qi zhuang zhuang huo shi qi
氣 食 少 火 壯 火 散 氣 少 火 生 氣
qi shi shao huo zhuang huo san qi shao huo sheng qi
A strong fire decreases the *qi*, a gentle fire strengthens the *qi*; a strong fire feeds on the *qi*, the *qi* feed on a gentle fire; a strong fire dispels the *qi*, a gentle fire produces the *qi*.

All cooks will recognize what is said here. When there is too much heat, either for a casserole or for the body, it will destroy the tastes and produce an unpleasant smell of burning, whilst a gentle fire helps things to cook: all the ingredients mix and create a good aroma.

A gentle fire recalls both the fire of *mingmen*, which maintains all the vital functions, and that of the triple heater. A powerful fire blazes in a way that is harmful. The fact that this warning is inserted here also makes us think that it is addressed to therapists who are too quick to stimulate the *yang* in their patients and to prescribe remedies which stimulate the *yang*, without realising that an excess of *yang* can be as fatal as an excess of *yin* or a deficiency of *yang*.

21. 氣味辛甘發散為陽酸苦涌泄為陰
qi wei xin gan fa san wei yang suan ku yong xie wei yin

As to *qi* and tastes, pungent and sweet, which cause things to burst forth and spread out, are *yang*; sour and bitter, which cause things to rise up and be eliminated, are *yin*.

The discussion here is not concerned with laying down practical rules for treatment or for the composition of remedies, but with presenting large-scale models of *yinyang*.

The *qi* and the tastes taken together have different qualities of *yang* or *yin*. Reference should be made to Suwen Chapter 22 for the *yinyang* characteristics of the five tastes. Here we have only four of them, according to the pattern of the four seasons: *yang* of *yang*, *yin* of *yang*, *yang* of *yin*, *yin* of *yin*.

The different *yang* energies express themselves in various ways, from pouring forth and diffusing, to inducing sweating (*fa san* 發散), just as the different effects of *yin* range from moving upwards to eliminating (*yong xie* 涌泄). Vomiting is the effect of a movement upwards, and purging the action of evacuating. In the last two cases, condensed matter, substances, are worked upon, representing a *yin* effect. When this effect is pure, it reveals itself as purging, and when it is mixed with *yang*, it becomes vomiting.

22. 陰勝則陽病陽勝則陰病
yin sheng ze yang bing yang sheng ze yin bing

When *yin* prevails, *yang* is diseased, when *yang* prevails, *yin* is diseased;

Too strong a *yang* damages *yin*; a dominant *yin* weakens *yang*.

23. 陽 勝 則 熱 陰 勝 則 寒
yang sheng ze re yin sheng ze han
When *yang* prevails, there is heat, when *yin* prevails, there is cold;

This is a further example of the *yinyang* couple as a model for heat and cold. Having dealt with tastes, which come from the earth, it is now the turn of external influences, the *qi* of heaven affecting the human being, to give life, maintain life or to attack. Cold will reflect the qualities of *yin*, heat those of *yang*, each at its particular level and according to its nature.

24. 重 寒 則 熱 重 熱 則 寒
zhong han ze re zhong re ze han
Increasing cold results in heat; increasing heat results in cold.

By analogy, the same mechanisms are at work within the seasons of heaven as in the human body. Terrestrial *yin* and *yang* (*qi* and tastes) form various substances which take their places in space; heavenly *yin* and *yang* (atmospheric agents) form the moments of time and their successive cadences.

The couplings based on *yinyang* serve as a basis for the division into five. Thus tastes, like atmospheric agents, are usually presented in terms of five. This is an exposition of the doctrine of *yinyang* and the five elements.

25. 寒 傷 形 熱 傷 氣
han shang xing re shang qi
Cold injures the form, heat injures the *qi*.

Cold, being *yin*, adds to the condensation of the body, and easily attacks what is fundamentally of the same nature as itself. Heat, being *yang*, is attracted by the *qi*, which reflects a *yang* model.

We could find any number of examples here, for instance that cold attacks the body more superficially, whilst heat is created more easily in the interior. It is just as easy to find examples of the opposite, for instance that of cold attacking the *qi* internally. We can observe and describe the interlocking of *yin* and *yang* in a living body at many different levels.

26. 氣 傷 痛　形 傷 腫
qi shang tong xing shang zhong
Injury to the *qi* gives rise to pain, injury to the form gives rise to swelling.

Yang, which is dilute and subtle, has no form, nor do the *qi*; and pain, although real and actually experienced, in itself has no form. Pain, which is a disturbance of natural exchanges and circulations (both at the mental and the physical level), is an excellent example of the manifestation of an attack upon the *qi*.

The body is a form; any attack upon it will be visible and palpable. Swelling, which is an exaggeration of a shape for one reason or another, here above all from cold, is chosen as representing an attack upon the body.

27. 故 先 痛 而 後 腫 者 氣 傷 形 也 先 腫 而 後 痛 者 形 傷 氣 也
gu xian tong er hou zhong zhe qi shang xing ye xian zhong er hou tong zhe xing shang qi ye
Therefore, if there is first pain then swelling, the *qi* are injuring the form; and if there is first swelling and then pain, the form is injuring the *qi*.

Given the relationships between the body and the *qi* described above, attack upon one will have an effect upon the other.

28. 風 勝 則 動 熱 勝 則 腫 燥 勝 則 乾 寒 勝 則 浮
feng sheng ze dong re sheng ze zhong zao sheng ze gan han sheng ze fu
濕 勝 則 濡 瀉
shi sheng ze ru xie

If wind prevails, there is agitation; if heat prevails, there is swelling; if dryness prevails, there is drying out; if cold prevails, there is bloating; if dampness prevails, there is liquid diarrhoea.

After discussing the hot/cold coupling, we move on to the five atmospheric agents. Each is described both as an example of a pathological reaction as well as of an actual reaction, showing that the symptom described can actually occur. A typical example is then discussed, rather than moving on to analyse the different pathologies specific to the five elements.

Wind, which activates and moves, produces erratic movements expressing themselves as muscular spasms as well as bouts of anger. Heat, which degrades liquids, causes swellings full of pus to occur. Dryness destroys fluids and results in a lack of moisture. Cold weakens the *qi*, condensing humid vapours, which infiltrate the tissues causing superficial oedema. Dampness which has not been transformed in the interior of the body draws everything downwards, like a mudslide.

29. 天 有 四 時 五 行
tian you si shi wu xing
Heaven has four seasons and five elements

Heaven controls the unfolding of time and the relationships with the earth, and is the master of the seasons. Heaven also contains the models and patterns for the generation of beings on earth. The planets, each with its specific colour and circulation, manifest the five aspects of the vital movement in the heavens. On earth these are the five elements.

The seasons, which are never described as five in number, because the concept of 'four seasons' is too well-established, express the vision of the infinite multiplication of *yinyang* through the succession and interlocking of couples. To enable them to be brought into the theory of the five elements, they are associated here with the five elements present in heaven in such a way as to reveal the five different seasonal or climatic influences.

30. 以 生 長 收 藏
yi sheng zhang shou cang
For generating, growing, gathering and burying

These are the four movements and actions specific to each of the four seasons. The action of spring is to produce and generate, that of summer is to grow and mature, that of autumn is to gather and to harvest, and that of winter is to bury and store.

31. 以 生 寒 暑 燥 濕 風
yi sheng han shu zao shi feng
And to produce cold, heat, dryness, dampness and wind.

The five influences emanate from the four seasons and the five elements of heaven. This cleverly reconciles the four and the five, *yinyang* and the five elements. The seasons of heaven are sent towards the earth as a blending of five kinds of *qi*. These five kinds of *qi* are a way to speak of all the qualities of the *qi* of heaven.

32. 人 有 五 藏 化 五 氣
ren you wu zang hua wu qi
Human beings have five *zang* and, through transformation, five *qi*,
Human beings are manifested entirely on this model of five. They have five *zang*, which are the expression of the five elements and the five aspects of vital movement. The five *qi* represent these vital movements, resembling the atmospheric agents which emanate from the five elements in heaven. Human beings evolve within the environment of the four seasons.

33. 以生喜怒悲憂恐
yi sheng xi nu bei you kong
Which produce elation, anger, sadness, oppressive grief and fear.

These *qi* represent the profound life emanating from the *zang*, they describe the emotions and tendencies specific to each *zang*, which we recognize as the five expressions of will (*wu zhi* 五 志). They will be presented later as being able to reach the *zang* itself directly, whilst the tastes and atmospheric agents first reach the body form.

The comparison of human emotions and dispositions with celestial meteorology forms part of the Chinese tradition, of which the beginning of Zhuangzi chapter 2 is one of the first examples. We can also refer here to Laozi chapter 23, The Chunqiu Zuozhuan, Duke Zhao 1st Year (see Wu Xing, Monkey Press 2008), and above all to Huainanzi chapter 7 (see Jing Shen, Monkey Press 2010).

34. 故 喜 怒 傷 氣 寒 暑 傷 形
gu xi nu shang qi han shu shang xing
Thus elation and anger injure the *qi*, cold and heat injure the form.

The same reasoning by analogy is followed here, this time focused on physiological and pathological implications. Emotions, all of which are represented here using the example of the *yinyang* coupled emotions of anger and elation, are primarily disturbances of *qi*, and are deviations from the appropriate movement. They therefore affect the sources of power which control these movements, which are the *zang*. External forms of aggression, represented by the coupling of cold and heat, are first felt in the body and then in the storehouses of vital energy.

35. 暴 怒 傷 陰
bao nu shang yin
Violent anger injures the *yin*,

Anger represents the *yang* within the movements of the emotions, and destroys the *yin*. Violent anger is caused by a contra-flow of rising *qi* which carries blood upwards, damaging and draining the kidneys and the *yin*, which are below.

36. 暴 喜 傷 陽
bao xi shang yang
Violent elation injures the *yang*.

Elation represents the *yin*, too much of this movement injures the *yang*. Excessively strong elation stimulates movement towards the exterior, causing an escape of vital energy through shouting, gesticulation, and sweating. Such inappropriate actions lead to exhaustion and loss of energy and also the voice.

37. 厥 氣 上 行 滿 脈 去 形
jue qi shang xing man mai qu xing
When *qi* rise up in reverse, they congest the vital circulation and leave the body.

In the network of vital circulation, blood and *qi* become blocked, congesting certain areas while others are depleted; this will be reflected in the pulse. Blood-and-*qi* no longer circulate normally in the *mai* (vital circulation); essences and spirits no longer support each other. The vital spirits no longer manifest themselves, and the movement of life is interrupted, remaining only in an inert shape, without the pulsation of life.

38. 喜 怒 不 節 寒 暑 過 度 生 乃 不 固
xi nu bu jie han shu guo du sheng nai bu gu
If elation and anger are not well regulated, if cold and heat are excessive, life is no longer secure.

The external pathogenic agents, like internal emotional disorders, weaken the flow of life and its resistance to harmful influences. We must develop an understanding of how to maintain life, if we are to live a good and long life. (cf. Lingshu chapter 8, Zhuangzi chapter 3)

39. 故 重 陰 必 陽 重 陽 必 陰
gu zhong yin bi yang zhong yang bi yin
So increasing *yin* turns into *yang* and increasing *yang* turns into *yin*.

This restates an idea already discussed at the beginning of this chapter in order to provide examples from pathology. *Yin* generates *yang* and *yang, yin*; pathogenic agents relating to a specific season will cause illnesses of another kind to occur in the following season.

40. 故曰冬傷於寒春必溫病
gu yue dong shang yu han chun bi wen bing
Therefore it is said, injury by cold in winter leads to warm diseases in spring.

Using the example of a specific pathogenic process, that of winter cold blocking the circulation and causing heat as a reaction, we are shown how cold produces heat and how the cold pathogenic factor, in the cold season, thus double cold, causes warm diseases (*wen bing* 於 寒), once spring arrives (cf. Suwen chapter 3).

41. 春 傷 於 風 夏 生 飧 泄
chun shang yu feng xia sheng sun xie
Injury by wind in spring leads to diarrhoea with undigested food in summer.

Wind, by nature formless and active, *yang* and linked with wood, attacks the spleen-earth causing illnesses characterized by an outflow of damp due to loss of the movements and functions of the spleen.

There is incomplete transformation, since food is not well-digested, and transportation is no longer controlled, as shown by the occurrence of diarrhoea. Since the examples relate to the four seasons, the spleen and humidity appear in the summer, which is to be taken here as being the end of summer.

42. 夏 傷 於 暑 秋 必 痎 瘧
xia shang yu shu qiu bi kai nüe
Injury by heat in summer leads to intermittent fevers in autumn.

Summer heat which is not eliminated hinders the movement of autumn, which refreshes and retreats. The opposition of these two contrary movements causes intermittent fevers (cf. Suwen chapter 2).

43. 秋 傷 於 濕 冬 生 咳 嗽
qiu shang yu shi dong sheng ke sou
Injury by dampness in autumn leads to coughing in winter.

Dampness prevents the lung from distributing the *qi* in an orderly way. Winter cold intensifies this inability to the point where the contra-flow in the *qi* leads to coughing.

44. 帝 曰 余 聞 上 古 聖 人 論 理 人 形 列 別 藏 府 端 絡 經 脈
di yue yu wen shang gu sheng ren lun li ren xing lie bie zang fu duan luo jing mai
The Emperor said, I was taught that the sages of ancient time presented the principles organising the human body, ordering and differentiating the *zang* and the *fu*, determining the extremities and branchings of the meridians,

This describes the acute insights of the sage who observes the universal norms of life, as manifested in human beings. The *zang* and *fu* organs form the knot of life. They control its first impulse, which is internal and hidden, and is differentiated into many specific expressions of the original *qi*. The *zang* and the *fu* are organized and differentiated in the body according to the pattern of *yinyang* and the five elements.

The organs form the centre of life, from whence it spreads in all directions, guided by the meridians. The extremities of the vertical axis are carefully fixed at top and bottom, and the branches are grafted to left and right on to the trunk of the meridians (*jing mai* 經 脈), until they fill the whole vital space of the body with circulations which connect with one another (the *luo* 絡).

45. 會 通 六 合 各 從 其 經
    hui tong liu he ge cong qi jing
Grouping them together to ensure free communication in the six junctions, each according to its proper norms;

A clearly defined whole is formed and delimited by the relationships and communications which maintain it. Six junctions (*lui he* 六 合, cf. Suwen chapter 6) represent the totality of vital exchanges. These exchanges are organized by rules which are the meridians (*jing* 經). Each portion of the space and time of the body obeys, by affinity, a precise quality of *qi* provided and controlled by the meridian.

46. 氣 穴 所 發 各 有 處 名
    qi xue suo fa ge you chu ming
Assigning to each cavity of *qi* that springs forth a location and name;

The internal activity rises towards the surface where 'holes' or 'points' can be felt; these are the places where specific forms of *qi* can be adjusted. Each of them is identified by a specific location and name.

47. 谿 谷 屬 骨 皆 有 所 起
    xi gu shu gu jie you suo qi
Recognising how activity arises from the ravines and the valleys,

and the bones which support them;

Form emerges from what is unformed through pathways which provide access and connections within the mass of the flesh (ravines and valleys, *xi gu* 谿谷). Circulations and activities form the relief of the landscape. The bones support and guide the form of the flesh as well as the meridians which control circulation. The bones also support the muscular force which moves the flesh.

48. 分部逆從各有條理
    fen bu ni cong ge you tiao li
Giving to each well-divided region, with its currents and counter-currents, the principle of organisation;

What comes from the depths controls what is at the surface. The quality of *qi* and fluids reaching the external areas of the body makes the skin smooth and supple, its texture firm and the pattern of its lines correct. In return, the proper maintenance of the surface prevents leakage and loss which may harm and diminish the inner richness of *qi* and fluids, as happens for instance in the case of profuse sweating.

49. 四時陰陽盡有經紀
    si shi yin yang jin you jing ji
Giving the *yinyang* of the four seasons the cycles of its regular course;

Time is merely the regular unfolding of the seasons and of their subdivisions, seen in cyclical terms.

50. 外內之應皆有表裡
    wai nei zhi ying jie you biao li
Recognising all the outward and inward exchanges in the correspondences between the exterior and the interior.

In the body space (external and internal, *wai nei* 外 內), the exchanges between outside and inside (*biao li* 表裡) help to distinguish the visible (the surface) from the invisible (what is inside), and make it possible to perceive what is active as an expression of what is latent.

其 信 然 乎
qi xin ran hu
Are we really to put our faith in that?

51. 岐 伯 對 曰
Qi bo dui yue
Qi Bo replied:

Qi Bo's reply discusses the organization of the universe according to the five aspects of vital movement. Each is described under twelve headings (*jie qi* 節 氣), which show how the *qi* manifests itself in its various aspects; each quadrant is a quality of the terrain, created by the earth under the influence of heaven. The particular quality of the earth, in this place, draws a heavenly *qi*, an atmosphere, to it, by affinity.

Life is created on earth from this embrace, and is characterized by an element. A taste structures the beings thus created, and makes it possible for us to detect the quality of their essences. In human beings, a *zang* reproduces the power of the element, and is formed and then maintained by the taste which corresponds to it.

In the body structure, the *zang* creates a form and action which are more external. In their diversity and their unity, the passages of the essences and the vital spirits, which form the upper orifices, reflect what distinguishes the five *zang* and what draws them together.

Here the five heavenly *qi* are presented as atmospheric agents:
- the five elements of the earth;
- the five levels contained within the body structure (*ti* 體);
- the five *zang*;
- the five colours (*se* 色), which are the impressions which the

eye receives of the external projection in colour of the authentic substance of a being.
- the five tones (*yin* 音), which are the impressions the ear perceives, the brain registers and the heart understands, and which distribute all that vibrates according to five modalities. These vibrations cannot be seen, palpated, felt or tasted. They are hardly 'heard', but, if our heart is pure, they teach us something about the essence of situations and beings.
- the five sounds (*sheng* 聲) are a more sensitive and more defined resonance than that of a 'tone'. They express the passage of *qi* in the instrument created by the human body, particularly the heart and the windpipe.
- five different reactions to a deterioration in the normal functioning of a *zang* (*bian dong* 變 動) at a deep level. If things become abnormal, the movement becomes sensitive and the mechanisms of the body malfunction.
- the five sense organs, the upper orifices;
- the five tastes;
- the five aspects of will, which represent vital tension differentiated in the body according to five poles. They are expressed in the form of a related grouping of feelings, each rooted in its natural place, the *zang*.

If the will belonging to a *zang* becomes disturbed, it loses its control over the feeling which animates it and expresses it. As was discussed earlier, the emotions affect the *zang* directly, bringing disorder to the control which it exercises over the *qi* of life.

As a result of the play of affinities and the productive cycles (or cycles of control, *ke*) within the five elements, an uncontrolled emotion will be brought back to a state of greater balance by the emotion representing the contrary movement which balances and controls it. But it is more a matter of balance within the *qi*, than the interplay of different emotions.

When the atmospheric agents are pathogenic, they attack the body structure at the exterior, according to their respective affinities and attractions. The pathogenic agent will be controlled by its opposite –

always at the level of the interaction of the five *qi* or the five elements. When tastes are pathogenic, that is to say excessive, they also first affect the body structure. The opposite taste re-establishes balance.

52. 東 方 生 風
dong fang sheng feng
The eastern quarter produces wind,

The east (*dong* 東) represents the visible upsurge of life (spring, sun), the agitation of vital movement everywhere. Wind (*feng* 風) is a sign of movement taking place, of *qi* awakening and animating the great mass of the earth, which carries away and sows the seeds of life.

53. 風 生 木
feng sheng mu
Wind produces wood,

Wood (*mu* 木) rises up, supple and strong, like a tree which draws on its sap and its roots to raise itself towards the heights, to enable its branches to spread out and stir in the wind.

54. 木 生 酸
mu sheng suan
Wood produces the sour,

The sour taste (*suan* 酸) pierces strongly through the hardest substances, and directs this power inwards. Wood represents the violence of all beginnings.

55. 酸 生 肝
suan sheng gan
Sour produces the liver,

In human beings, the liver (*gan* 肝) represents a rising movement, a movement of upsurge, release, momentum; impetuous but controlled diffusion towards the periphery, stirring up and stimulating. It spreads out as a function of the richness and solidity of the base upon which it rests.

56. 肝 生 筋
gan sheng jin
The liver produces muscular movement,

Muscular force (*jin* 筋) owes its strength to its solid foundation upon bone, and its impregnation with blood and nutrients, which are impelled inwards through the action of the liver.

57. 筋 生 心
jin sheng xin
Muscular movement produces the heart;

This refers to the productive cycle (*sheng* 生), in which wood is represented by the muscular force, fire by the heart. Muscular force can also be regarded as the basis for the movement of the heart, just as wood is the impulse given to the expansion of fire.

58. 肝 主 目
gan zhu mu
The liver masters the eyes.

The eye (*mu* 目) directs the brilliance of its gaze into the distance, reaching the far confines of the world. This represents the power of diffusion and the furthest point to which the body's orifices extend. It is an expression of the powerful spreading of the wood.

59. 其 在 天 為 玄 在 人 為 道 在 地 為 化
qi zai tian wei xuan zai ren wei dao zai di wei hua
化 生 五 味 道 生 智 玄 生 神
hua sheng wu wei dao sheng zhi xuan sheng shen

In heaven, it is the deep mystery, in humans it is the *dao*, on earth, it is transformation.
Transformation produces the five tastes, the *dao* produces wisdom, the deep mystery produces the spirits.

This paragraph is introduced here as part of the presentation of the east (and not in the following sections) to add weight to the impulse of life represented by the east. In six phrases the text reminds us that we can discover the manner in which life unfolds and that the web of the universe is organized according to five modalities, so that we can act effectively, and the human spirit receive what is necessary to bring contentment. All this rests firmly, however, upon a deeper mystery. Inexpressible, ineffable in itself, it is seen in the three powers of the world: heaven, earth and human being.

Heaven acts as initiator beyond the individual form of things, concealing the mystery of life which is expressed as the spirits in each person (*shen* 神). The earth shapes and transforms, differentiates and diversifies. It forms and maintains individual lives through the tastes and their alchemy. A model for human life is thus laid down, according to which the individual nature is adapted to the particular circumstances of existence. The task is to learn what to do to follow one's own path, and accomplish one's personal destiny. This is the way (*dao* 道).

By looking at how human perception, starting with the mystery of the origin of all things, organizes the five great axes around which all phenomena are grouped, we can better understand what underlies the movements of beings and things, better know how to act, for ourselves and for others, in order to live and allow others to live in harmony.

60. 神 在 天 為 風 在 地 為 木 在 體 為 筋 在 藏 為 肝
shen zai tian wei feng zai di wei mu zai ti wei jin zai cang wei gan
在 藏 為 肝 在 色 為 蒼
zai zang wei gan zai se wei cang

The spirits! In heaven are wind, on earth are wood, of the parts of the body are muscular movement, of the *zang*, the liver, of colour, green-blue.

Greenish-blue (*cang* 蒼) is the colour of heaven, the reservoir and source of life.

61. 在 音 為 角
zai yin wei jue
Of musical tones, it is *jue*,

The tone *jue* is a vibration which 'regularizes and straightens', and which encourages kindness and humanity. When it is disturbed, it expresses an oppressive and uneasy sadness. It affects the liver much more directly, rapidly and profoundly than the sour taste. It can stimulate the liver's own properties or overwhelm them.

Jue is not only a tone, or a mode or musical note; it also represents all kinds of ambience, atmospheres, feelings or perceptions of the world around us, which are perceptible by no other recognized sense.

62. 在 聲 為 呼
zai sheng wei hu
Of sounds, it is shouting,

A shout (*hu* 呼) is sharp and loud, and caused by expelled air, as when we breathe out. It is a kind of noisy rush of wind which we expel, particularly when we are making an effort. It is the sound of the newborn baby, or of the woman in labour and caused by violent muscular exertion, or anger.

63. 在 變 動 為 握
zai bian dong wei wo
Of reactions to change, it is contraction,

Constriction (*wo* 握) here means any form of contraction or clenching. It is a sign of an attack upon the liver within the muscles.

64. 在 竅 為 目 在 味 為 酸 在 志 為 怒
zai qiao wei mu zai wei wei suan zai zhi wei nu
Of orifices, it is the eyes, of tastes, it is sour, of expressions of will, it is anger.

Anger (*nu* 怒) represents the impetuosity of life itself, the power of its beginnings, the force of that which pushes and pierces through to enable the day to appear. If unleashed uncontrollably, it creates imbalance in the exchanges and circulation of blood-and-*qi* by pushing the vital energy too strongly upwards. (cf. The Seven Emotions, Monkey Press)

65. 怒 傷 肝 悲 勝 怒
nu shang gan bei sheng nu
Anger injures the liver, sadness prevails over anger;

There is a kind of psychological appropriateness in this almost mechanical application of the *ke* cycle. Sadness (*bei* 悲) reduces the *qi*, and draws together the system by which the heart is connected to the rest of the body. The *qi* is no longer diffused, movement is interrupted and the balance between blood-and-*qi* is disturbed.

Sadness acts like an extinguisher placed over the pointed flame of anger. But this is not a kind of cheap psychology – above all it is a matter of *qi*, and how to effectively regulate the powerful *qi* of wood within the emotions.

66. 風 傷 筋 燥 勝 風
feng shang jin zao sheng feng
Wind injures muscular movement, dryness prevails over wind;

Wind, like anger, is a powerful pathogenic factor for the liver, because the place where something is at its most powerful is where it is also at its most vulnerable; we are most profoundly affected by something which affects us most closely and intimately.

The liver cannot exist without wind and anger but they must be under its control. For example, a good general has a strong temperament and may easily be impetuous – his courage is his strength, but he may become too aggressive. If wind or anger are not in control, the process becomes pathological. It is easy to understand, therefore, that wind disturbs the liver, creating disorder in the balance between blood and *qi*, and causing erratic movements in the muscles, such as cramps and convulsions.

It is less easy to understand how dryness controls wind. This is an example of too systematic an application of the *ke* cycle. This difficulty will be resolved with respect to other applications without bringing in the *ke* cycle (see note 112), but this cannot be applied to wind, because wind can reinforce the negative power of all the other agents. The power of the west is therefore simply shown as being capable of reducing that of the east – metal controls wood. Here dryness is merely the expression of the metal *qi*, as wind is the expression of the wood *qi*.

67. 酸 傷 筋 辛 勝 酸
suan shang jin xin sheng suan
Sour injures muscular movement, bitter prevails over sour.

Sour draws things together (cf. Suwen chapter 22). An excess of the sour taste inhibits the rooting of the liver in the *yin*, and stops the liver *qi* from expanding and spreading out, thus impeding the vital circulation which passes through the muscles. The bitter taste, on the other hand, controls what rises up and diffuses (Suwen chapter

22). It therefore encourages the flow and free circulation of body fluids, making for better irrigation of the muscles and relaxation of contractions.

68. 南方生熱
nan fang sheng re
The southern quarter produces heat

The south (*nan* 南) is the domain of luxuriant and abundant vegetation, of immense, burgeoning, age-old trees, of large birds, of heat and the abundance of *yang*. Life expands and multiplies everywhere.

Heat (*re* 熱) corresponds to this. It eases the circulation and the spreading out of all things. It helps them to mature and brings them to the fullness of their being, provided that excessive heat does not turn into a destructive furnace.

69. 熱生火
re sheng huo
Heat produces fire,

Heat in the *qi* of heaven is the element fire on earth. Fire has the same qualities as heat, reflected in the productive power of the earth. It is the infinite circulation of life which rises from the depths to spread out and fill all space.

70. 火生苦
huo sheng ku
Fire produces the bitter,

The bitter taste (*ku* 苦) determines the internal structure of all that is fashioned according the *qi* of fire.

71. 苦 生 心
ku sheng xin
Bitter produces the heart,

In human beings the heart (*xin* 心) assumes the role of the sovereign 'facing south' (cf. Suwen chapters 6 and 8). It spreads out the fire of life and the power and delight in living, which arise perpetually from the void of the heart, the dwelling place of the spirits, their best and only shelter.

72. 心 生 血
xin sheng xue
The heart produces blood,

The circulation of blood, the red liquid, reaches all parts of the body, bringing life to them and endowing them with the presence of the heart and its spirits. Perhaps the reason why blood is here preferred to *mai*, (脈) vital circulation, is because of the relationship of blood and spirits, which is mentioned frequently. *Mai* is the network that transports and circulates the blood to all parts of the body, and corresponds to heart-fire. It may also be because of the statement which follows, which says that blood is associated more with the spleen than with the *mai*.

73. 血 生 脾
xue sheng pi
Blood produces the spleen;

The renewal of blood mainly takes place between the spleen and the heart. The spleen provides rich fluids which form the basis of blood, and the heart imprints its seal upon them, giving them their true qualities. There is also a flow of blood back from the heart towards the spleen, which inspires it and supplies it with the *yang* and the heat necessary for it to carry out the movements that enable it to transport and transform.

74. 心 主 舌
xin zhu she
The heart masters the tongue.

The tongue manifests the qualities of subtlety and discernment which are qualities of the heart; it is what enables us to recognize the true taste of a substance. It is through the tongue that we can express the richness of the heart in words, that we state our opinions and that we voluntarily modulate our vital breath. This is carried out through the inspiration of the spirits.

75. 其 在 天 為 熱 在 地 為 火 在 體 為 脈
qi zai tian wei re zai di wei huo zai ti wei mai
In heaven it is heat, on earth it is fire, of the parts of the body, it is the vital circulation,

In this presentation of body parts, it is the *mai* (脈) which are mentioned, not blood, as above. They allow the circulation of the blood, and it is through their pulsations that they express the normal process of blood circulation and the balance between blood and *qi* inside these movements. They are thus a true expression of the *qi* of fire.

76. 在 藏 為 心 在 色 為 赤
zai zang wei xin zai se wei chi
Of the *zang* organs, it is the heart, of colours, it is red,

In all creatures which have blood, the natural red (*chi* 赤) colour is equivalent to the green of vegetation. It is the red of blood which brings a flush to a new-born baby's cheek, it is the colour of naked skin and of the heart. To the Chinese, the redder the heart, the more loyal and sincere a person is considered to be.

77. 在 音 為 徵
zai yin wei zhi
Of musical tones, it is *zhi*

The tone *zhi* (徵) is a vibration which creates harmony; it stimulates joy, even elation. When it is disturbed, it expresses distress, becoming a sorrowful and painful note of complaint.

People in a city emit a vibration which is perceptible to the sage. If he notices something in the general ambience which is analogous to the tone *zhi*, this warns him of approaching drought.

78. 在 聲 為 笑
zai sheng wei xiao
Of sounds, it is laughter,

Laughter (*xiao* 笑) is healthy and good when it expresses well-balanced feelings. It spreads from the heart, is formed, rises and bursts out from a state of peace, joy and serene elation. But it can also explode under the pressure of extreme excitement and agitation of the spirits, becoming wild, uncontrollable laughter which denotes an unhealthy internal state.

79. 在 變 動 為 憂
zai bian dong wei you
Of reactions to change, it is oppressive grief,

Grief (*you* 憂) describes a state of oppressive despondency, the opposite of that which circulates freely and unfolds at ease (cf. Lingshu chapter 8.) It is a sign of a weakness of the heart and the spirits, of the joy of life which they impart and of the communications made by the *mai*. Everything becomes heavy and sluggish, slows down and stagnates.

80. 在 竅 為 舌 在 味 為 苦 在 志 為 喜
    zai qiao wei she zai wei wei ku zai zhi wei xi
Of orifices, it is the tongue, of tastes, it is bitter, of expressions of will, it is elation.

Elation (*xi* 喜) is the gentle stimulation of the vital circulation arising from a feeling of freedom and well-being in the depths. Light and aerated blood circulates freely, leading to speed of thought and agility of movement.

81. 喜 傷 心 恐 勝 喜
    xi shang xin kong sheng xi
Elation injures the heart, fear prevails over elation.

If elation becomes exaggerated, it causes excitation and agitation which leads to loss of spirit and disrupts the proper conduct of life. Fear (*kong* 恐) causes things to draw inwards, counteracting the harmful effects of elation. But again elation and fear are here a representation of a particular kind of *qi*, rather than a specific emotion.

82. 熱 傷 氣 寒 勝 熱
    re shang qi han sheng re
Heat injures the *qi*, cold prevails over heat.

The *qi* are here regarded as the aspects of the body disturbed by heat, the atmospheric agent of the south. With respect to the heart, the body is therefore represented under three different aspects: the blood, the *mai* and finally the *qi*. The heart unfolds its power by means of this three-fold animation. The beginning of Suwen chapter 5 reminded us that too strong a fire destroys the *qi*, whilst moderate heat maintains and animates life. Cold reduces the effects of excessive heat quite naturally.

Another, more historical, explanation is that the text of Suwen chapter 5 is more of a collection of texts fom various origins. In the general presentation of the five elements we obviously have different texts, and the last one presents the relationship within the *ke* cycle. This last text certainly comes from a school in which *qi* are related to the fire and the south, and blood to water and the north.

83. 苦 傷 氣 鹹 勝 苦
ku shang qi xian sheng ku
Bitter injures the *qi*, salty prevails over bitter.

Again according to Suwen chapter 22, a bitter taste strengthens, drying up the penetrating dampness. A salty taste, which cools, softens and humidifies, corrects the harmful effects of excessive bitterness.

84. 中 央 生 濕
zhong yang sheng shi
The central region produces dampness,

The central region (*zhong yang* 中央) is the middle and the median of the four directions; it takes from the four quarters and gives back to them. It is without measurable size, and enables the passages, transitions, exchanges and permutations of all the qualities of *qi* to take place in harmonious acts of interpenetration. It is thus the supreme place where balance can be maintained. China, it must be remembered, is the country of the middle.

Dampness (*shi* 濕) is created by a balance of what is solid and what is liquid, a harmony between *yin* and *yang*. If there is too much dampness, everything will be soaked. If there is not enough, everything will dry out and wither. A beneficial level of dampness circulates in the form of vapour, penetrating everything and providing the necessary lubrication for movement and relationships to take place.

85. 濕 生 土
shi sheng tu
Dampness produces earth,

Dampness impregnates and fertilizes. It enables the soil to bind together and become fertile. It enables clay to be moulded into shapes, fields to be irrigated, and the 10,000 beings to prosper. The earth (*tu* 土) can thus receive all kinds of seeds and nourish them, supplying what is necessary for their successive acts of transformation. This is then redistributed to all, according to their needs and their affinities.

86. 土 生 甘
tu sheng gan
Earth produces the sweet,

Sweet (*gan* 甘) is the taste of a blend of the five grains produced by the earth. It is agreeable in the mouth, because it is a taste which does not produce an excessive reaction. The relationship between the taste of what is in our mouth and what we are is congruent. Because this taste is the combination of the five tastes, it is the taste which is able to create and impliment this link.

87. 甘 生 脾
gan sheng pi
Sweet produces the spleen,

The function of the spleen (*pi* 脾) is to receive and distribute everything. It is in charge of transformation, and ensures the proper assimilation, maintenance and continual reconstruction of life.

88. 脾 生 肉
pi sheng rou
The spleen produces the flesh,

Flesh (*rou* 肉), when abundant and opulent, is evidence of the fertility of the earth and the good condition of the spleen. It gives shape to the body as earth gives shape to the land. Just as the earth is furrowed by rivers and streams, so, too, is the flesh threaded through with currents and circulations which determine its outlines and animate it – on its surface and even more so deep within.

89. 肉 生 肺
rou sheng fei
The flesh produces the lung;

The *qi* are disseminated by the lung (肺), the master of *qi*, provided that the flesh opens up the pathways of circulation so that there is no obstruction to the proper cadence of their movement – then the lung can expand. In return, the power of these circulations gives cohesion to all the particles which form the mass of the flesh, drawn together by the relationships of the *qi*.

90. 脾 主 口
pi zhu kou
The spleen masters the mouth.

Food enters through the mouth (*kou* 口). But it is also the mouth from which sounds are emitted, revealing the internal vitality, both at its most mundane, in belching and vomiting, or at its most noble, with words and smiles. As an orifice, the mouth is a manifestation of the doubling of the centre; it is involved in the turbidity of food, but also enables the pure expression of the heart to vibrate through the tongue, as the spleen nourishes the heart.

91. 其在天為濕在地為土在體為肉
qi zai tian wei shi zai di wei tu zai ti wei rou
在藏為脾在色為黃
zai zang wei pi zai se wei huang

In heaven, it is dampness, on earth, it is the earth, of the parts of the body, it is flesh, of the *zang* organs, it is the spleen, of colours, it is yellow,

Yellow (*huang* 黃) is the colour of ploughed land, irrigated and penetrated by the luminous rays of what is fertile. Yellow (yellowish, earthy, clay-like) also reflects a mixture of all the colours produced on earth, whilst the sum of all the pure colours (light) produces white.

92. 在音為宮
zai yin wei gong
Of musical tones, it is *gong*,

The tone *gong* (宮) forms the foundation for the other tones, being the lowest pipe or sound. It is the first note of the scale, and represents the prince who from his central palace creates harmony for his people by his friendly and gentle behaviour, welcoming all to him.

93. 在聲為歌
zai sheng wei ge
Of sounds, it is singing,

Because of its harmony, continuity and rhythm, singing (*ge* 歌) expresses internal satisfaction and physical and mental contentment. It is also a way of relating to others, either through singing in unison or in turns.

94. 在 變 動 為 噦
    zai bian dong wei yue
Of reactions to change, it is belching,

Belching (*yue* 噦) indicates rejection, a refusal on the part of the earth – which should accept all. It can be good or bad, manifesting either repletion or the reaction to incomplete digestion, or a contra-flow in the *qi* of the stomach.

95. 在 竅 為 口 在 味 為 甘 在 志 為 思
    zai qiao wei kou zai wei wei gan zai zhi wei si
Of orifices, it is the mouth, of tastes, it is sweet, of expressions of will, it is thought.

Thought (*si* 思) is the collection and arrangement of assimilated memories, knowledge and impressions. It penetrates widely and deeply within us and within the nature of human beings. Nothing is beyond its remit, and it continually transforms these aspects of consciousness within us.

96. 思 傷 脾 怒 勝 思
    si shang pi nu sheng si
Obsessive thought injures the spleen, anger prevails over obsessive thought.

Thoughts which are obscured by unclear images and cannot be properly integrated or used to lead to effective action, turn into preoccupations. A thought which is fixed upon one aspect of feeling, upon one idea, turns into an obsession and the compulsion to repeat itself. It is opposed to the proper movement of the spleen.

Anger represents that which arises from the impetuous nature of of liver-wood, it pushes movement forwards, unblocking an obsessive situation, and making new arrangements of images and projects for the future (cf. Lingshu chapter 8).

97. 濕傷肉風勝濕
shi shang rou feng sheng shi
Dampness injures the flesh, wind prevails over dampness.

If dampness is not assimilated, it becomes excessive and destroys the firmness of the flesh and blocks circulation. Wind dries and moves; it dissipates dampness and gets the circulation moving again.

98. 甘傷肉酸勝甘
gan shang rou suan sheng gan
Sweet injures the flesh, sour prevails over sweet.

The sweet taste eases tensions in the circulation (cf: Suwen chapter 22), but excess sweetness creates a loosening or slackening which takes away the dynamic power from the vital circulation. The action of the sour taste is to draw things together, which compensates for this slackness.

99. 西方生燥
xi fang sheng zao
The western quarter produces dryness,

The west (西), where the sun sets, is a return, a descent, which translates itself in atmospheric terms into the effect of condensation. This condensation transforms light mist into drops of water. Where large drops of water fall, it can appear as humidity, or as dryness (*zao* 燥) in what had been impregnated by a fine humid mist. This loss of impregnation prepares the way for the separation of water and earth which is completed in winter (cf. Suwen chapter 2).

100. 燥生金
zao sheng jin
Dryness produces metal,

Metal (*jin* 金) is the prototype of condensed and dried matter within the heart of the earth. It represents form which is complete and hard. But it also represents the possibility of the loss of form, by melting down, which can then be followed by remaking as a new form. This smelting of the metal can go on indefinitely without the metal losing its quality or quantity – just as autumn is the season in which everything reaches its point of final maturity, only for it to be cut, destroyed or ingested.

101. 金 生 辛
jin sheng xin
Metal produces the pungent,

The punjent taste (*xin* 辛) evokes bitterness and suffering, the punishment of a rebel. Submission to the west or to autumn, which opens the way to death and the mysterious domain of the spirits, is not easy, just as the movement of the retreat of the *yang* towards the *yin* is not natural to us. Rebellion, which can manifest itself physically in intermittent fevers, bears its own punishment within it, for it will only bring pain. A similar impression is given by the punjent taste.

102. 辛 生 肺
xin sheng fei
Pungent produces the lung,

The lung (*fei* 肺) controls the condensation and downward pressure of fluids. It represents the diffusion of purified *qi*. Acting with the severity and rigour of metal, it regulates the circulation of *qi* and gives rhythm to the breath.

103. 肺 生 皮 毛
fei sheng pi mao
The lung produces skin and body hair,

Skin and body hair (*pi mao* 皮毛) represent the limit of the expansion of *qi*, as well as of the body. They regulate the rhythm of exchanges with the exterior and do not allow anything to disperse to the outside. They also prevent external influences penetrating within. They reflect the effects of the vitality of *qi* and of fluids coming from the interior at the extremity, and they initiate the return towards the interior of the elements responsible for the essences.

104. 皮 毛 生 腎
pi mao sheng shen
Skin and body hair produce the kidneys;

The kidneys (腎) benefit from this return movement from the frontiers of the body. They absorb the vitality in the depths, and being at the base of the trunk they also benefit from the movement of pressure applied upon fluids from above by the lung.

105. 肺 主 鼻
fei zhu bi
The lung masters the nose.

The nose (鼻) provides a passage for the *qi* of heaven, and thus for respiration. It does not cope well with blockages or the flow of unassimilated, unduly concentrated fluids. Among the orifices it reflects the characteristics of the lung.

106. 其 在 天 為 燥 在 地 為 金 在 體 為 皮 毛
qi zai tian wei zao zai di wei jin zai ti wei pi mao
在 藏 為 肺 在 色 為 白
zai zang wei fei zai se wei bai
In heaven, it is dryness, on earth, it is metal, of the parts of the body, it is the skin and body hair, of the *zang* organs, it is the

lung, of colour, it is white,

White represents all colours mixed together; they must be pure, just as the *qi* and fluids of the lung must be pure and maintain this purity. White also represents the splendour of the sun blinding us with its light, or that of the setting sun. White is therefore a colour which can evoke both purity and decline, and even death, being the colour of whitened bones in the earth, the whitening of hair, and of the brightness of weapons which kill or of tools which scythe.

107. 在 音 為 商
zai yin wei shang
Of musical tones, it is *shang*,

The second tone *shang* (商) is a sound which is light, strong and metallic; it is drawn out and expands. Because of the clarity of its initiation, the sound spreads far and wide into the distance. This tone is associated with the ministers who serve the prince. They must be implacable, but have integrity, to ensure that the necessary duties are taken on, but are not experienced as too onerous by the people.

108. 在 聲 為 哭
zai sheng wei ku
Of sounds, it is sobbing,

A sob (*ku* 哭) suggests mourning and sadness. The tempestuous rising of *qi* and fluids – which block the throat, change the sounds of the mouth, and disturb the balance of the *qi* and of fluids in the nose and eyes – are often the effect of sadness.

109. 在 變 動 為 咳
zai bian dong wei ke
Of reactions to change, it is coughing,

Coughing (*ke* 咳) is the manifestation of the incapacity of the lung to ensure the regulation of *qi*, of their rhythm and proper propagation.

110. 在竅為鼻在味為辛在志為憂
zai qiao wei bi zai wei wei xin zai zhi wei you
Of orifices, it is the nose, of tastes, it is pungent, of expressions of will, it is oppressive grief.

Grief (*you* 憂) is a form of oppression, when it takes too tight a stranglehold over movement it prevents the distribution of *qi*.

111. 憂傷肺喜勝憂
you shang fei xi sheng you
Oppressive grief injures the lung, elation prevails over oppressive grief.

Grief of this kind extinguishes the *qi* through overuse. Joy rekindles the flame and enables life to re-start in the veins and in the heart.

112. 熱傷皮毛寒勝熱
re shang pi mao han sheng re
Heat injures the skin and body hair, cold prevails over heat.

Here we have heat (*re* 熱) when we would expect dryness (*zao* 燥). If we were to apply the concept of the control cycle mechanically, however, heat could be said to re-establish balance when there is an excess of dryness. This is, however, impossible. Heat is therefore chosen to evoke a hot dryness which removes the oiliness from the skin-and-hair, a reminder that, if the heat of summer lasts into autumn, this is an indication that there has been no inward-turning movement appropriate for this season. Cold, which is the opposite of heat, brings the situation back into balance.

113. 辛傷皮毛苦勝辛
xin shang pi mao ku sheng xin
Pungent injures the skin and body hair, bitter prevails over pungent.

That which is pungent encourages things to flow and diffuse (Suwen chapter 22), creating humidity and lubrication. For example, eating a fresh pepper will cause tears to flow. If there is an excess of the pungent taste, everything becomes unrestrained and in disarray; everything moves to the exterior, which can appear as excessive joy or abundant sweating, and this leads to an impoverishment within. A bitter taste is used to provide a foundation for the *qi* and help consolidate their position, since it has a strengthening and reducing action.

114. 北方生寒
bei fang sheng han
The northern region produces cold,

The north (*bei* 北), the region of the obscure and of *yin*, a place of exile where communication is disrupted, is also the place which harbours the hidden reserves necessary for the fermentation of life. It provides evidence of renewal. The cold (*han* 寒), which freezes relationships and offers the greatest risk to the *yang* of life, is also that which draws together and encloses. That which acts as a kind of firm separation can also offer protection as the need arises.

115. 寒生水
han sheng shui
Cold produces water,

Water (*shui* 水) is the source of life. When it flows gently, it can gives rise to all forms of change. When it is persistent, it always reaches where it has to go (cf. Huainanzi chapter 1). In its liquid form, water penetrates the depths of the earth or flows towards the sea. As vapour, it forms the clouds in the heavens or penetrates within compact masses. As ice, it blocks but also protects.

116. 水 生 鹹
shui sheng xian
Water produces the salty,

The salty taste (*xian* 鹹) is that of water which has become brackish as it is absorbed in the ground, like rock salt. It is also the taste of sea water.

117. 鹹 生 腎
xian sheng shen
Salty produces the kidneys,

The salty taste penetrates the kidneys by affinity, enabling them to reconstitute themselves and re-assemble their power and the movement characteristic to them.

118. 腎 生 骨 髓
shen sheng gu sui
The kidneys produce bone and marrow,

The kidneys work on the power of fluids in the depths of the body in order to attain suppleness and strength. The dual nature of the kidneys appears in the dual aspect of the body structure associated with them; the thick fluid of the marrow (*sui* 髓) gives the bones (*gu* 骨) their firmness and straightness, and the solidity of the bones retains the fluidity of the marrow within them.

119. 髓 生 肝
sui sheng gan

Marrow produces the liver;

The marrow (髓) expresses the *yin*, representing the water of the kidneys. This acts as a foundation for the liver, in form of the blood which it stores. The liver can then realize its *yang* effects.

120. 腎 主 耳
shen zhu er
The kidneys master the ears.

The ear (*er* 耳) captures sounds and sends them deep within. In normal circumstances, it is an orifice which prevents anything from escaping to the outside. The similarity in the nature of ears, kidneys and beans is reflected in their similar shape.

121. 其 在 天 為 寒 在 地 為 水 在 體 為 骨
qi zai tian wei han zai di wei shui zai ti wei gu
在 藏 為 腎 在 色 為 黑
zai zang wei shen zai se wei hei
In heaven, it is cold, on earth, it is water, of the parts of the body, it is bone, of the *zang* organs it is the kidneys, of colours, it is black,

Black (*hei* 黑) reminds us of deep water, the darkness of the night and the north; also of soot which is the trace left behind by fire. Black is the colour of that which lacks *yang* to enable it to circulate properly, as is the case with stagnant blood, for example.

122. 在 音 為 羽
zai yin wei yu
Of musical tones, it is *yu*,

The sound of the fifth tone *yu* (羽) is deep and serious. As an expression of harmonious power it represents an abundance of vital reserves. When it is disturbed, it reveals anxiety and deficiency.

123. 在 聲 為 呻
zai sheng wei shen
Of sounds, it is sighing,

A sigh (*shen* 呻) is the result of an internal dilation, an extension of *qi* rising from below. In normal circumstances, *qi* under control creates a kind of sing-song note, which is a deep form of breathing. As a sign of disturbance, it represents the effort made to remove an obstruction in the base of the trunk.

124. 在 變 動 為 慄
zai bian dong wei li
Of reactions to change, it is shivering,

A shiver (*li* 慄) is caused by trembling from cold, the result of weakness of the *yang* of the kidneys and thus of the defensive network, or by fear, caused by a deficiency in the kidneys' power of retention.

125. 在 竅 為 耳 在 味 為 鹹 在 志 為 恐
zai qiao wei er zai wei wei xian zai zhi wei kong
Of orifices, it is the ears, of tastes, it is salty, of expressions of will, it is fear.

Fear (*kong* 恐) is a movement downwards, a folding inwards into the depths. In normal circumstances it counteracts excitement, impetuousity and an outward-turning movement.

126. 恐 傷 腎 思 勝 恐
kong shang shen si sheng kong

Fear injures the kidneys, thought prevails over fear.

Excessive fear leads to hasty flight. Essences escape through the lower orifices, the whole body is in flight. There are movements and actions associated with panic, which are no longer controlled by the proper coordination between the kidneys and the heart, between the essences and the spirits. This is because the essences exaggerate the downward pressure and are unable to communicate with the spirits in the upper heater.

Reflective thought (*si* 思) represents the movement of the centre as it re-establishes the exchanges between what is above and what is below – returning to their centre those who have lost possession of themselves, and restoring stable reflection, which is the only thing capable of removing fear.

127. 寒 傷 血 燥 勝 寒
han shang xue zao sheng han
Cold injures the blood, dryness prevails over cold.

Dryness (*zao* 燥) replaces dampness (*shi* 濕), which would balance the cold in accordance with the control cycle. Cold and dampness are usually considered to be the same in nature (*yin*), and are therefore unable to control each other effectively, whereas dryness can more easily be associated with *yang*. This is, however, an unsatisfactory statement, and is there more for the sake of symmetry than for any practical application, but it is also the possible result of ancient associations.

The other inconsistency in this systematic exposé, that which replaces bones and marrow with blood (below) is, however, significant. Blood represents the marriage of water (liquid) with fire (the colour red). It is the essential fluid of the body and therefore belongs to the kidneys. In addition, since the *qi* are in the heart, the place which corresponds to the presentation of the south, this is another example of the *yinyang* coupling of the kidneys and heart, water and fire, and blood and *qi*. This is a further reference to the presence of this fundamental coupling in the presentation of the five *zang* and the five quarters. (cf. note to line 82)

128. 鹹傷血甘勝鹹
xian shang xue gan sheng xian
Salty injures the blood, sweet prevails over salty.

The salty taste makes things supple and soft, but too much salt dries the blood by thickening it. The sweet taste (*gan* 甘) increases fluids, particularly those which are *yin* in nature. It moves quickly, has little density and circulates rapidly; restoring the flow of fluids eliminates dryness and thirst.

129. 故曰天地者萬物之上下也
gu yue tian di zhe wan wu zhi shang xia ye
Thus it is said: heaven and earth are the high and the low for the ten thousand beings

Beyond the four quarters which divide earth and distribute its qualities, heaven and earth produce the mass of the world by calling endlessly upon what is above and drawing up constantly what is below. The great rhythmic and circulating movements within each of us play out through these rises and falls.

130. 陰陽者血氣之男女也
yin yang zhe xie qi zhi nan nü ye
And *yinyang* the male and female for blood and *qi*

Human beings are both male and female, the difference between them being the result of the specific regulation of blood and *qi* for each sex. Men and women mix the essential qualities of their *yinyang*, their blood and *qi*, to form something unique and produce a new life.

131. 左右者陰陽之道路也
zuo you zhe yin yang zhi dao lu ye
Left and right the paths and routes for *yinyang*

From day to day, life is regulated by the balance of left and right. Assuming that one is facing south, the left is sunrise and the side of *yang*, of rising up and of activity; the right is sunset and the side of *yin*, of descent and of rest. At each moment, specific hierarchies determine anew what is left and what is right in terms of social order and relationships (cf. Granet, The Right and the Left).

132. 水火者陰陽之徵兆也
shui huo zhe yin yang zhi zheng zhao ye
Water and fire the expression and revelation of *yinyang*

Water and fire are the intermediaries between that which has no form and that which has form (cf. Huainanzi chapter 1). *Yin* and *yang* have no particular form, but penetrate and give form to every being which has form. Water and fire are the first agents of vital change. They cannot be defined by a specific form, but leave specific impressions which can be gauged by touch and by the other sense organs.

133. 陰陽者萬物之能始也
yin yang zhe wan wu zhi neng shi ye
Yinyang is the power and the beginning of the ten thousand beings.

Male and female, and all that is in their image, are situated in relation to one another between heaven and earth, and reproduce heaven/earth, enabling the changes created by water and fire to be made and life to be maintained, within them and for them, as well as by them. This represents the power of life, which is always available and waiting to manifest itself. It moves itself and moves us towards a beginning; it is unique in itself but perpetually renews itself.

134. 故曰陰在內陽之守也陽在外陰之使也
gu yue yin zai nei yang zhi shou ye yang zai wai yin zhi shi ye

So it is said: *yin* is on the inside but *yang* keeps it there; *yang* is on the outside but *yin* sends it there

Yin qi, which are internal, enable *yang qi* to act as guard and defence. *Yang qi*, which are on the outside, enable *yin qi* to make use of their help (cf Suwen chapter 3). *Yin* and *yang* only create life and the maintenance of life when they act together. Nutrition and defence, marrow and bone, are examples of this synergy.

135. 帝曰法陰陽奈何
di yue fa yin yang nai he

The Emperor asked: What is the norm in terms of *yinyang*?

136. 岐伯曰陽勝
qi bo yue yang sheng

Qi Bo replied: When *yang* prevails,

This illustrates the progression of a pathological state due to the domination of *yang*, a harmful effect caused by fire and heat, which can ultimately cause *yin* to disappear, and death to occur.

137. 則身熱腠理閉
ze shen re cou li bi

The body heats up and the pores of the skin close,

The feeling of heat comes from the power of *yang qi* and its movement towards the interior. Fluids are transformed into hot steam which burns itself out. The reduction in humidity leads to a loss of the lubrication needed to open and close the pores. Because of this lack of suppleness and the drying out of fluids, the features become drawn and the passages blocked.

138. 喘粗為之俛仰
chuan cu wei zhi fu yang
Noisy and laboured breathing causes the head to droop and lift,

Heat affects both the back and the front of the body. On the thorax, it hinders the descending and regulating of the *qi* under the influence of the lung, causing dyspnoea due to a counter-flow, and the harsh noises caused by blocked *qi* in the chest. Breathing may be improved by moving the chest back and forth, and the head up and down.

139. 汗不出而熱
han bu chu er re
Sweat cannot escape and heat becomes intense,

Because the pores of the skin, *cou li* (腠理) are closed, heat cannot escape through sweat, remaining instead dammed up in the body where it grows more and more intense.

140. 齒乾
chi gan
The teeth dry out,

Heat which cannot escape penetrates more and more deeply inside the body. If it reaches the stomach, it appears in the mouth as the 'drying out' of the teeth. More seriously, if it dries out the essences of the kidneys, it damages the lubrication of all the bony structures of the body, of which the teeth are the external manifestation.

141. 以煩冤
yi fan yuan
One suffers from burning disease,

At an even more profound level, the blood and the spirits of the heart are affected, leading to disturbances and troubles which are no longer simply physical but emotional.

142. 腹 滿 死
fu man si
The abdomen is congested and death ensues.

At its most intense, heat causes bloating and swelling of the stomach, leading to blockage of the circulation. *Yang* is everywhere, forcing *yin* out from all areas of the body. Death is inevitable.

143. 能 冬 不 能 夏
neng dong bu neng xia
It is possible to survive in winter, but not in summer.

When *yin* has dried up, winter can come to our aid, and can lead to remission, but when the heat of summer arrives, it adds to the internal troubles, and resistance is no longer possible.

144. 陰 勝 則 身 寒 汗 出
yin sheng ze shen han han chu
When *yin* prevails, the body becomes cold and sweats,

Because the defensive system has become weakened, the *yang* no longer carries out its role of maintaining the *yin*. The pores open because there is a lack of tension, and allow cold sweat to escape.

145. 身 常 清
shen chang qing
The body is permanently frozen,

The *biao* (表), the outer surface of the body, the layers of skin and of the flesh, suffer from the reduction in heat carried by the *qi*. Cold creeps in, and there is insufficient strength to heat things up internally.

146. 數 慄 而 寒
shuo li er han
Shaken by shivering, the cold intensifies;

Shivering indicates that the cold has penetrated deep inside and that the body is trying to rekindle the movement of the *qi*.

147. 寒 則 厥
han ze jue
The cold causes weakening,

Yang has now completed its decline, internally as well as externally. It can no longer expand outwards, and this weakening of the body's defences and absence of the correct *qi* leads to reversal (*jue* 厥).

148. 厥 則 腹 滿 死 能 夏 不 能 冬
jue ze fu man si neng xia bu neng dong
The abdomen becomes congested; death ensues. It is possible to survive in summer, but not in winter.

The cold now blocks the circulation. Everything becomes frozen and fixed, nothing can move and death ensues. In both cases, there is the same final symptom, stomach congestion which prevents movement and transformation. There is no renewal of vitality as it is impossible to draw upon the original resources, which create life.

此 陰 陽 更 勝 之 變 病 之 形 能 也
ci yin yang geng sheng zhi bian bing zhi xing neng ye
These are the changes according to the contrasting prevalence of *yin* and *yang*, revealing the manifestation and virulence of diseases.

149. 帝 曰 調 此 二 者 奈 何 岐 伯 曰 能 知 七 損 八 益
di yue tiao ci er zhe nai he qi bo yue neng zhi qi sun ba yi
The Emperor asked: How are these two set right?
Qi Bo replied: If one knows the seven decreasings and the eight increasings,

The 'seven decreasings' (*qi sun* 七損) and the 'eight increasings' (*ba yi* 八益) represent fluctuations in the vital current, in a normal as well as a pathological situation. Thus, the Taisu explains the symptoms of death caused by the prevalence of *yang* or *yin* as being an application of the seven decreasings and eight increasings. There are, however, many other interpretations, particularly in relation to sexuality, and of course the seven and eight year cycles of fertility described in Suwen chapter 1. The general meaning is to be able to follow the rise and fall in natural strength, in order to maintain a harmonious balance. This is not the same balance in summer as in winter, in youth as in old age, for a man as for a woman or during the day as at night. The most appropriate *yinyang* balance must be found for each occasion.

150. 則 二 者 可 調
ze er zhe ke tiao
One is able to regulate both;

It is finding this balance that leads to a long life. It is in the ability to re-establish this balance in those who have lost it that the art of the true therapist lies. This means to be in possession of the necessary skill and knowledge.

151. 不 知 用 此 則 早 衰 之 節 也
bu zhi yong ci ze zao shuai zhi jie ye
But acting without this knowledge one declines prematurely.

Nothing good will be achieved by applying these formulae and techniques, even if they are well tried and tested, if we do not make a correct assessment of what is appropriate for that particular situation. It is dangerous to always want to add something, just as it is harmful, sometimes even fatal, to reduce at the wrong time. Knowledge comes from knowing how to use all the techniques for reducing and increasing, such as sedation and tonification, fasting and dietary considerations, and sexual, gymnastic and alchemical practices at the appropriate time.

152. 年 四 十 而 陰 氣 自 半 也 起 居 衰 矣
nian si shi er yin qi zi ban ye qi ju shuai yi
At forty, *yin qi* are reduced by half, activity declines;

According to Suwen chapter 1, human beings start to decline at 40 (the fifth period of 8 years for a man, or for a woman the fifth period of seven years, 35). This reversal of the vital processes starts internally, as the kidneys lose their power, the essences no longer create as much *qi*, the authentic fluids dry up and the original reserves weaken– the process starts with the *yin*.

A man of 40 begins to be less active during the day, and his activities lose some of their power. He sleeps less and rests less at night, and this trend gradually increases (cf. Lingshu chapter 18). The decline will be all the quicker if he takes no account of the new *yinyang* balance and tries to use his energy as before.

153. 年 五 十 體 重 耳 目 不 聰 明 矣
nian wu shi ti zhong er mu bu cong ming yi
At fifty, the body is heavy, the ears and eyes have lost their quickness and sharpness;

Movements become slower, the release of *qi* becomes weaker, centrifugal diffusion to the layers of flesh lessens. Clear *yang* rises towards the head, the orifices become deprived of essences, and the capacity of the sense organs lessens. The individual becomes heavier and moves increasingly less, and at the same time the sharpness of the mind declines, becoming less and less capable of taking in (by sight and hearing) what is happening outside – or even to be interested in this.

154. 年 六 十 陰 痿 氣 大 衰 九 竅 不 利 下 虛 上 實
    nian liu shi yin wei qi da shuai jiu qiao bu li xia xu shang shi
    涕 泣 俱 出 矣
    ti qi ju chu yi

At sixty, the *yin* is impotent, the *qi* decline greatly, the nine orifices lose their ease of function, there is emptiness below and fullness above, nasal mucus and tears flow out.

The *yin* becomes increasingly incapable of supporting the *yang*. This affects sexuality more specifically, but also all the different functions of the body, and resonates throughout the vital circulation. The weakening of the essences and reduction in *qi* affect both the lower and upper orifices. It becomes more difficult for things to pass through them, because the capacity to transport and transform has decreased.

Fluids, which are poorly assimilated and retained because of the lack of *yang*, of fire, escape from the orifices. This happens more from the upper orifices, indicating an inappropriate fullness at the top of the body, whilst there is draining below, as the fundamental forces of life become exhausted.

155. 故 曰 知 之 則 強 不 知 則 老
    gu yue zhi zhi ze qiang bu zhi ze lao

Thus it is said: The strength of those who know will be maintained; ageing will occur in those who do not know.

The vital processes proceed without obstruction and without exhaustion in those who know how to conduct themselves and know how to act and to live. Such people do not impede what takes place, either physically or emotionally, nor do they exhaust themselves in vain by opposing what is happening.

Those who do not know how to conduct themselves are blocked

everywhere, and their life force is expended in inappropriate behaviour.

156. 故 同 出 而 名 異 耳
gu tong chu er ming yi er
Thus, 'Coming from the same origin, they will still have different names.'

This is a direct quote from Laozi chapter 1. It reminds us that the opposite and complementary aspects of all things come from the same source and are differentiated only in the forms they take.

157. 智 者 察 同 愚 者 察 異
zhi zhe cha tong yu zhe cha yi
Where those who have true knowledge see sameness, those who do not know see difference.

Sameness (*tong* 同) refers to what things originally have in common. To be able to see what is alike is to trace sufficiently far back to find what unites two different situations. It is not to dwell upon, and even less to become fixed upon, the differences in their expression. The *dao*, or the life process, is one; it is the unity of all that exists, but its expressions and manifestations are many. The ten thousand beings give rise to envy. They oppose one another and compete with one another, sometimes they disagree with one another and contradict one another. But they must never exclude one another, since they are born from the same mother and each express an aspect of what exists. To be truly effective practitioners, we have to be able to trace back to the roots of the illness (cf. the beginning of chapter 5). True knowledge is that which bases itself upon the origin of beings. All knowledge and all applications of knowledge which claim to be able to do without this, lead to false conclusions, and will at some point lead to serious failure.

158. 愚者不足智者有餘
yu zhe bu zu zhi zhe you yu
Those who do not know always lack something, while those who know have in abundance,

When knowledge is not based upon the source of life, this leads to a search for formulae and procedures which are always partial, inadequate and unsatisfactory both for the practitioner and for the patient. It leads to a constant search for more, because what is given does not respond to the real need. It is useless to attempt to treat and heal a human being while ignoring the profound needs of human life. This is represented by an individual *yinyang* combination and the maintenance of constant exchange and renewal, and also by a presence illuminated by the spirits, which cast light upon the relevance of this *yinyang* combination and inspire the correct way of thinking, and the correct relationships, gestures and activities.

The practitioner who adheres to these essentials may struggle and suffer, but will experience a degree of satisfaction that cannot be diminished. The practitioner who refuses to do this, may accumulate any number of patients or wealth, but the heart will hunger after true fulfilment.

159. 有餘則耳目聰明身體輕強
you yu ze er mu cong ming shen ti qing qiang
老者復壯壯者益治
lao zhe fu zhuang zhuang zhe yi zhi
An abundance which appears as sharpness and quickness of ears and eyes, and an alert and robust body. Even when old, their vigour returns to them, a vigour which enables them to conduct their life perfectly.

Those who want to renew and guard the essences and *qi*, enable their spirits to regulate their life by a sense of omnipresence in each area of their being. They waste nothing, and use their faculties to perfection. They thus increase their knowledge and their strength indefinitely, these being totally interdependent when they are true to themselves.

The upper orifices, saturated with essences, animated by *qi* and inspired by the spirits, perceive with clarity and precision, and enable a reliable image of reality to be reflected back in the heart. The heart can receive impartially, without reaction, and therefore embody this true knowledge. This enables blood and *qi* to receive the best effects of organic life, because the spiritual aspects of life are now secure.

160. 是 以 聖 人 為 無 為 之 事 樂 恬 憺 之 能
shi yi sheng ren wei wu wei zhi shi le tian dan zhi neng
從 欲 快 志 於 虛 無 之 守
cong yu kuai zhi yu xu wu zhi shou

This is why the sages practised doing by non-doing, delighting in their capacity for quiet and serenity, they followed their desires and benefited from their will, remaining within emptiness and nothingness.

故 壽 命 無 窮 與 天 地 終 此 聖 人 之 治 身 也
gu shou ming wu qiong yu tian di zhong ci sheng ren zhi zhi shen ye

Therefore, long life enabled them to accomplish their destiny, without limitation, sharing with heaven and earth until the end. This is how the sages conducted their lives.

There is no difference between perfect health and the state of sagehood or wisdom. All that is needed is to follow one's nature, which means to know and to recognize it, to correct the deviations and perversions of the body, of the emotions and of the perceptions of the heart, so as to reject what is harmful – which is whatever is against our true nature.

Having reached this state of alignment, the desires of the heart or the conduct of life are no different from the natural vital pulsation of life which expresses itself fully. This is acting without acting (*wei wu wei* 為無為), the emptiness of the heart and serene ease.

161. 天不足西北故西北方陰也
tian bu zu xi bei gu xi bei fang yin ye
而人右耳目不如左明也
er ren you er mu bu ru zuo ming ye

Heaven is deficient in the north-west, therefore the western and northern quarters are *yin*, and in man ear and eye are not as clear on the right as on the left.

地不滿東南故東南方陽也
di bu man dong nan gu dong nan fang yang ye
而人左手足不如右強也
er ren zuo shou zu bu ru you qiang ye

Earth is not full in the south-east, therefore the eastern and southern quarters are *yang*, and in man hand and foot are not as strong on the left as on the right.

In ancient times, heaven and earth remained in balance with one another, separate but connected together by eight giant pillars. Neither the heavenly vault nor the surface of the earth tilted to one side or the other, and the world was then completely stable. But a monster broke the north-western pillar, which was never completely repaired again. Since then, heaven inclines towards the north-west and earth towards the south-east. The sun, moon and stars which follow the movements of the heavens move towards the north-west, the confines of space where the planes of heaven and earth draw together, whilst rivers and streams follow the inclination of the earth, and flow towards the south-east, where all the waters pour into the deep abyss, at the point where the planes of heaven and earth are the furthest from one another. Where the plane of heaven or of earth tilts downwards is where their power weakens.

The human body reflects this model, with its *yinyang* crossing between heaven and earth. The most perfect human being is the one at the median point, reflecting the relationship of heaven and earth at its most subtle and graceful. An imbalance between the *qi* of *yinyang* will appear as some constitutional imbalance.

The upper body, typified by the roundness of the head, with its clear and subtle orifices, is the moving image of the power of the *qi* of heaven. The lower part of the body, which bears the limbs and touches the ground through the square of the two feet, is a moving reflection of the power of the *qi* of the earth.

Thus heaven declines towards the north-west where the *yang* is deficient and the *yin* prevails, and it is cold and dark. What is *yang* and heavenly in the human body will lack power in relation to what corresponds to the north-west, which is on the right side, reflecting both the decline of *yang* and sunset.

Earth is weaker in the south-east, where *yin* is deficient and *yang* prevails, and it is hot and bright. What is *yin* and of the earth in the human body will lack power in relation to what corresponds to the south-east, which is on the left side, the rise of *yang* and sunrise.

162. 帝曰何以然
di yue he yi ran
The Emperor asked: How is this?

岐伯曰東方陽也陽者其精并於上
qi bo yue dong fang yang ye yang zhe qi jing bing yu shang
并於上則上明而下虛
bing yu shang ze shang ming er xia xu
Qi Bo replied: The eastern quarter is *yang*, with *yang* the essences accumulate above; by accumulating above, what is above is resplendent and what is below becomes empty.

故使耳目聰明而手足不便也
gu shi er mu cong ming er shou zu bu bian ye
This gives sharpness and quickness to ear and eye, while hand and foot do not function as they should.

There is a tendency for clear *yang* to rise on the left side of the body, for what rises does so on the left, on the *yang* side. The pure essences generally move upwards, but the movement will be greater on the left, and the top of the body is therefore richer on the left. What descends will, however, be weaker on the left, and the lower areas will therefore have less essences and *qi*.

163. 西方陰也陰者其精
    xi fang yin ye yin zhe qi jing
    并於下并於下則下盛而上虛
    bing yu xia bing yu xia ze xia sheng er shang xu

The western quarter is *yin*, with *yin* the essences accumulate below; by accumulating below, what is below flourishes and what is above becomes empty.

故其耳目不聰明而手足便也
gu qi er mu bu cong ming er shou zu bian ye

Therefore ear and eye have neither sharpness nor quickness, while hand and foot function as they should.

The tendency for things to descend will be the opposite – on the right.

164. 故俱感於邪其在上則右甚在下則左甚
    gu ju gan yu xie qi zai shang ze you shen zai xia ze zuo shen

Thus, where there is a reaction to the perverse, above the right side is the most affected, but below the left side is the most affected.

This feature of the human constitution can be observed in pathological conditions as well as in practice. Immunity comes from a state of balance and regular functioning, whereas any excess of *yin* or *yang*, however slight, represents a potential danger.

165. 此天地陰陽所不能全也故邪居之
    ci tian di yin yang suo bu neng quan ye gu xie ju zhi

Because the *yinyang* of heaven and earth itself cannot be whole, the perverse find a place to settle.

There remains one question. Can a truly authentic human being make up for these defects and acquire the same sharpness of senses on the left and on the right, and the same power in the four limbs? The Taisu has no hesitation in stating that the authentic human being is perfect, and retains no trace of the misfortune which brought heaven and earth slightly into imbalance with one another; having returned to a point of original perfection.

166. 故 天 有 精 地 有 形
gu tian you jing di you xing
Thus heaven through its essences and earth through its forms,

The visibility of forms (*xing* 形) belongs to earth, in contrast to the mystery of the essences (*jing* 精) which belong to heaven. The essences are the seeds of life, which rule over the formation of the body and provide its outlines. They inspire each specific form whilst maintaining a power of life which belongs to no particular form. This is why, in the coupling created by essences and forms, the essences are associated with heaven and forms with earth.

167. 天 有 八 紀 地 有 五 理
tian you ba ji di you wu li
Heaven through the eight regulators and earth through the five organizers,

The eight regulators (*ba ji* 八紀) are the eight major calendar divisions of a year which regulate time: the equinoxes and solstices and the quarter days which begin each season – the beginning and mid point of each season. In the totality of time, heaven distributes its animating *qi*, determines the seasons and their internal changes, and establishes the balance of the year.

The five organizers (*wu li* 五理) are the five elements, the five-fold path through which the earth, replying to the demands of heaven, organizes life.

168. 故 能 為 萬 物 之 父 母
gu neng wei wan wu zhi fu mu

Can act as father and mother to the ten thousand beings.

Human beings are formed from the interaction of essences and *qi* regulated by heaven with the formative and structuring power of the earth.

169. 清 陽 上 天 濁 陰 歸 地 是 故 天 地 之 動 靜
qing yang shang tian zhuo yin gui di shi gu tian di zhi dong jing
神 明 為 之 綱 紀
shen ming wei zhi gang ji

Since clear *yang* rises to heaven, and turbid *yin* returns to earth, heaven and earth move and are still, the radiance of the spirits forms the net of laws and principles.

The median is animated by the nature of the two poles, as is the *yinyang* alternation which is always organized around a central power created by the spirits and their ability to expand. The detail of each life and the web of each incarnation are knitted together with reference to this centre which controls the expression of *yinyang*.

170. 故 能 以 生 長 收 藏 終 而 復 始
gu neng yi sheng zhang shou cang zhong er fu shi

Thus, through a process of generating, growing, gathering and burying, everything reaches its term and starts again.

Any fruit produced by the earth remains faithful to the organization and structure that the earth has given to it, and is subject to the majestic rhythms of heaven, obediently reflecting the movements of the seasons which modulate appearances and disappearances according to a rhythm of four beats – generation, growth, gathering in and burying.

171. 惟 賢 人 上 配 天 以 養 頭
wei xian ren shang pei tian yi yang tou
Only the wise, above, make themselves companions of heaven to maintain the life of the head;

To make oneself a companion of heaven is to be associated with the virtue of heaven, formed of expansive *yang*, of bright light and of pure essences. The head is given the clear *yang* that it needs, and the brain and sense organs draw to themselves the essences which are bearers of the radiant light coming from the spirits.

172. 下 象 地 以 養 足
xia xiang di yi yang zu
Below, make themselves into the image of earth to maintain the life of the feet;

To make oneself in the image of earth is to reproduce in the most complete way the models of stability and consistency the earth lays down. Our legs can never achieve the speed of thought or eye, but the human plant is well rooted by its limbs and by everything which circulates within it.

173. 中 傍 人 事 以 養 五 藏
zhong bang ren shi yi yang wu cang
In the middle, they occupy themselves with human affairs to maintain the life of the five *zang*.

When we deal with human affairs we are immersed in the world of relationships. The five *zang* are specific to human beings, and through their perfect balance, human beings are the most complete creation that exists between heaven and earth, fulfilling in exemplary fashion the role of the median point. Maintaining the five *zang* leads to a life coordinated in perfect balance with regard to all relationships, whether those we have outside ourselves, in human society, or, by analogy, those within ourselves, through the harmony of essences and *qi*. By regulating intake of food through the five tastes, the human being is constitutionally able to integrate all things. By maintaining balance in the intensity of desires, and in the pure and subtle tension which emanates from the *zang* – forming the psychic make-up and spiritual life – it is possible to move towards the state of the 'authentic human being' as seen in Suwen chapter 1, The Way of Heaven.

174. 天 氣 通 於 肺
tian qi tong yu fei
The *qi* of heaven commune with the lungs,

The lung, which is the highest organ in the body, is responsible for respiration, through which the *qi* of heaven are absorbed by the body. The interpenetration between the lung and the *qi* of heaven is written into our very nature. The dome formed by the two lobes of the lung draws the clear *qi* and controls their diffusion. The pure vapours which have risen upwards condense and fall as rain towards the base of the trunk. The lung is of course vital for the metabolism of fluids and the circulation of liquids as well as for the dissemination of *qi* throughout the body. (cf: The Lung, Monkey Press, 2001)

175. 地 氣 通 於 嗌
di qi tong yu yi
The *qi* of earth commune with the throat,

The food provided by the earth passes through the throat, to be absorbed by the body. Its *yin* nature and downwards movement, helped by the stomach, offset the *yang* expansion of the *qi* of the lung.

176. 風 氣 通 於 肝
feng qi tong yu gan
The *qi* of wind commune with the liver,

The liver, reflecting the wind, releases activity, in an impetuous bounding forward which allows things to surge, creating the force of movement.

177. 雷氣通於心
lei qi tong yu xin
The *qi* of thunder commune with the heart,

Thunder startles us awake and penetrates deep within the earth, shaking human beings from their drowsiness. In this it resembles the fire of the sun which lights up life, the fire which animates and re-animates. The heart, like thunder, although apparently silent, has the power to move and summon all the areas of the body to life. In China, as in many other civilisations, thunder is the sign of the force of the powerful, of the fear they inspire, but also of the benefits and challenges they offer to their inferiors.

178. 谷氣通於脾
gu qi tong yu pi
The *qi* of the valleys commune with the spleen,

Valleys are the passages through which all that maintains life circulates, whether these are the spaces between the mountains on earth or those between the masses of the flesh. The spleen is responsible for transporting and distributing the *qi* of cereals (*gu* 穀) which grow in the valleys (*gu* 谷).

179. 雨氣通於腎
yu qi tong yu shen
The *qi* of rain commune with the kidneys.

The analogy of rain and water recalls the rain of the kidneys which control the fluids in the body.

180. 六 經 為 川
liu jing wei chuan
The six meridians are like rivers,

The uninterrupted circulation of the meridians drains all the blood and *qi*. These control the supply of all that is necessary for maintenance, as a hydraulic network provides the necessary irrigation of the soil for things to grow and survive. Like rivers, the meridians vary in their flow at different points in time (cf. Suwen chapter 26); they also differ from one another, and place their own imprint upon each territory they pass through. The direction and orientation of their circulation within a specific territory fix its limits, ensuring that nourishment is brought to it and that it is defended, in the same way as the great arteries or roads on earth.

181. 腸 胃 為 海
chang wei wei hai
The intestines and stomach are like seas,

Seas are the collecting points for fluids which are waiting to move on again. They receive all the rivers of the earth, and through evaporation, form the clouds of heaven. The stomach and intestines receive all food, and through transformation draw from it what can be assimilated and distributed throughout the body.

182. 九 竅 為 水 注 之 氣
jiu qiao wei shui zhu zhi qi
The nine orifices are like *qi* pouring forth as water.

Pouring forth (*zhu* 注) indicates the power of the *qi* animating the fluids. *Yinyang* exchanges in the body are made through the orifices. Water and fire must balance themselves here. The fluids irrigate, enabling the movement of *qi* to take place through transformation. To enable an orifice to function, fire, which is an internal radiation outwards, must manifest itself within the fluids or the essences, culminating in the animation of the spirit. By affinity, in the upper orifices, fire and the spirits interpenetrate the essences to illuminate them and enable them to function with subtlety. But it is still essential for the fluids which cannot be taken up by the lower orifices to be eliminated.

Thus each being is a manifestation of *qi* within the *qi* of heaven, a tiny drop of liquid drowned in the ocean. Free and vital circulation takes place between the air which has been kindled, and the waters of the abyss – supreme archetypes of heaven/earth, where the rigid structures of a constant, totally reliable, universal order express themselves with the ease of the spontaneity which characterizes life. Atmospheric agents and earthly configurations intermingle here to enable them to exchange their influences. From head and foot, to the five *zang*, human beings correspond to this, creating free shapes from the shapes imposed upon them. This is a description of the animation of human beings within the universal flow of things.

183. 以 天 地 為 之 陰 陽 陽 之 汗 以 天 地 之 雨 名 之
yi tian di wei zhi yin yang yang zhi han yi tian di zhi yu ming zhi

In considering *yinyang* in its relation to heaven and earth, sweat is called *yang*, taking its name from the rain of heaven and earth.

There is no phenomenon within us which does not resonate with, and correspond to, heaven/earth. Sweat pours from the layers of the skin, which are hot and as though pulsing at the exterior. Sweat is a fluid which comes from the body's *yin*, and which flows over the body under the action of *yang qi*, just as rain is a fluid which arises originally from the earth as a result of evaporation, and flows along its surface under the impulse of heaven. Like rain, sweat maintains the body's heat, expels miasms and cleans the internal passages. Alternatively it can drain vitality and essences, or stagnate where it should flow, in a way that is harmful to the body.

184. 陽之氣以天地之疾風名之
yang zhi qi yi tian di zhi ji feng ming zhi

Qi is called *yang*, taking its name from the rapid wind of heaven and earth.

In ancient times, the concept of *qi* was so closely associated with the wind that the two were almost identified with one another. The rapid diffusion of *yang qi* in the body evokes the power of the wind, which spreads far and wide and occupies space, infiltrating everything. Overstimulation by the *yang* drains vitality, as does overstimulation by the wind. From being a source of life and movement, the wind may end up depriving us of both.

185. 暴氣象雷
bao qi xiang lei

When *qi* is violent, it takes on the image of thunder,

The violence of anger and that of violent muscular contractions and sudden outbursts of rage evoke a clap of thunder.

186. 逆氣象陽
ni qi xiang yang

When it runs counter to its proper course, it takes on the image of *yang*.

The exaggeration of the rising movement of *yang*, which pushes the *qi*, carrying the mass of blood upwards, is a prototype of counter-flow. When things flow against the current (*ni* 逆), this does not simply mean that they go in the opposite direction. Often it means that the natural rhythm is no longer maintained, even though the movement is in the same direction, it is not flowing correctly. An upward contra-flow can therefore be due to overstimulation of *yang qi*, or the incapacity of *yin* to retain the *yang* which then escapes.

187. 故 治 不 法 天 之 紀 不 用 地 之 理 則 災 害 至 矣
    gu zhi bu fa tian zhi ji bu yong di zhi li ze zai hai zhi yi

Therefore, to treat without the regulators of heaven as model and ignoring the organizers of earth, leads to disaster and catastrophe.

We can treat ourselves and be treated if we harmonize ourselves continually with heaven/earth. This *yinyang* model is the most perfect and the most obvious one there is, and acts as a reference point in us, explaining why imbalance occurs.

188. 故 邪 風 之 至 疾 如 風 雨
    gu xie feng zhi zhi ji ru feng yu

Perverse winds occur with the violence of a storm.

The key term describes a patient's inability to recover from imbalance by themselves, and is the starting-point of a presentation of a therapist's work. Wind is a way of describing all the harmful influences, suggesting the strength and speed of an attack which takes place without forewarning.

189. 故 善 治 者 治 皮 毛 其 次 治 肌 膚 其 次 治 筋 脈
    gu shan zhi zhe zhi pi mao qi ci zhi ji fu qi ci zhi jin mai
其 次 治 六 府 其 次 治 五 藏 治 五 藏 者 半 死 半 生 也
    qi ci zhi liu fu qi ci zhi wu zang zhi wu zang zhe ban si ban sheng ye

Thus he who excels in the art of healing will first treat the skin and body hair, then treat at the surface of the flesh, then treat the muscular movement and vital circulation, then treat the six *fu*, then treat the five *zang*; in treating the five *zang*, half will die and half will live.

He who excels in the art of healing can at first glance see the slightest imbalance before disease has become too established. A superficial treatment will then be enough, requiring little effort to achieve a simple result. This is where the great skill lies. Such a practitioner can treat at the level of skin-and-hair, because he can see what has not yet manifested itself. At each stage in the evolution of an illness, the treatment required is a function of the depth at which the attack has taken place. The process can be fast or slow, and an assessment of the depth of the attack forms part of the art of diagnosis.

The patient is weakened and the illness entrenched when harmful energies are deep, at the level of the *zang*, and there is less possibility of offering protection and restoring balance. Even an excellent practitioner will then only be able to save one patient out of two.

190. 故天之邪氣感則害人五藏
gu tian zhi xie qi gan ze hai ren wu zang
Thus when the perverse *qi* of heaven affect man, they harm his five *zang*;

Perverse atmospheric agents harm vital movements controlled by the five *zang*, wind harms the liver, heat the heart. Subtlety, absence of form and fundamental animation are the province of the *qi* of heaven as they are of the *zang*. When they are not in balance with one another, the *qi* of heaven harm the *zang*.

191. 水穀之寒熱感則害於六府
shui gu zhi han re gan ze hai yu liu fu
When heat and cold, due to liquid and solid food, affect man, they harm his six *fu*;

Because of its irregularities, solid food grown in the earth may have an irritating effect upon the body's receptacles for it, which are the six *fu*.

192. 地之濕氣感則害皮肉筋脈
di zhi shi qi gan ze hai pi rou jin mai
And when the damp *qi* of earth affect man, they harm his skin, flesh, muscular movement and vital circulation.

Humidity rises from the ground and impregnates the body. By impeding circulation, particularly that of the *yang* defensive *qi*, it successively harms the different levels of the body structure as it penetrates. This third attack – dampness at the centre, exchanges blocked through excess, stagnation of the *yin* and *yang* circulation – is typical of what occurs at the centre. It is also typical of what comes from the earth, just as the first is typical of what comes from heaven.

193. 故 善 用 鍼 者 從 陰 引 陽 從 陽 引 陰
gu shan yong zhen zhe cong yin yin yang cong yang yin yin
Thus he who excels with needles draws *yang* from *yin* and *yin* from *yang*.

This describes all the ways in which *yin* and *yang* cross in the body, such as the techniques for treating a meridian by its coupled meridian and treating the upper part of the body by the lower.

194. 以 右 治 左 以 左 治 右
yi you zhi zuo yi zuo zhi you
He treats the left side on the right and the right side on the left.

This describes, for example, the techniques of *miu* (繆) puncture, which are used for an attack at the level of the *luo* (絡), or the great puncture (*ju ci* 巨 束), which are used for an attack at the level of the meridians.

195. 以 我 知 彼
yi wo zhi bi
Through what is his, he reaches the other.

If a practitioner is to excel in treating with needles, having a good technique alone is not enough. He must also be deeply established within himself. This is what is needed to touch another. The richness of the relationship between the therapist and the patient, which is so important in traditional medicine, is only effective if the practitioner is able to understand the profound, true and therefore ineffable reality through the medium of himself.

196. 以 表 知 裡
yi biao zhi li
Through the manifest he reaches the inner organization.

By reading what is manifest on the outside, the surface, (*biao* 表), the great practitioner recognizes the exact nature of the internal reality (*li* 裡), with respect to what is normal for that person as well as what deviates from it or distorts it.

This reveals itself through clinical symptoms and signs as well as through the configuration of the body and general attitude. Structures are internal areas where vitality expresses itself and organizes itself at an invisible level.

197. 以 觀 過 與 不 及 之 理 見 微 得 過
yi guan guo yu bu ji zhi li jian wei de guo
Merely by observing what causes excess and what is deficient, he perceives what is most subtle and reveals what is not right.

The terms exceeding (*guo* 過) and failing to achieve (*bu ji* 不及) describe all the different nuances relating to fullness and emptiness which can be observed, first as they start to make themselves felt imperceptibly and then as they start to take hold.

198. 用 之 不 殆
yong zhi bu dai
His art is always faultless.

He who treats what is scarcely perceptible, by interpreting the signs correctly, and by applying appropriate techniques in just measure, can never err.

199. 善 診 者 察 色 按 脈 先 別 陰 陽
shan zhen zhe cha se an mai xian bie yin yang
He who excels in diagnosis examines the complexion and takes the pulse, above all to assess *yin* and *yang*.

The close relationship of blood and *qi*, and the balance of *yin* and *yang*, can be observed in the complexion and on the pulse, in two different and complementary ways, rising up from within and appearing on the surface of the body (cf. Suwen chapter 10). These observations can be refined even more by comparing the results of the examination of the complexion and pulse to see whether they match each other (a favourable prognosis) or whether they contradict one another (an unfavourable prognosis).

200. 審 清 濁 而 知 部 分
shen qing zhuo er zhi bu fen
He locates where there is a problem by assessing what is clear and what is turbid

Here, clear (*qing* 清) and turbid (*zhuo* 濁) describe the colours of the complexion, which can be luminous or dark. Bright colours indicate a *yang* disease, and dark colours a *yin* disease. A clear, oily complexion indicates relatively superficial pathological changes, where *qi* and blood will not suffer further, illness is then at the level of the *yang*. A dark complexion, particularly when it is accompanied by dryness, denotes deep and severe changes affecting essences-and-*qi*. Illness here is at the level of the *yin*. In addition, the specific area of the face where the complexion has changed informs us about the site of the illness, and in particular tells us whether it is the *zang* or the *fu* which have been affected (cf. Lingshu chapter 49).

201. 視 喘 息 聽 音 聲 而 知 所 苦
shi chuan xi ting yin sheng er zhi suo ku
He perceives where there is disease by assessing difficulties in breathing and listening to sounds and noises.

After a visual examination, the sounds and noises the patient emits are listened to. Apart from respiration, and the diagnostic indications which it offers, the practitioner listens to the sound of the voice, to all the noises emitted by the body and those already seen as related to each *zang*: shouting, laughing, sobbing, sighing and groaning.

202. 觀 權 衡 規 矩 而 知 病 所 主 按 尺 寸
guan quan heng gui ju er zhi bing suo zhu an chi cun
He perceives what is controlling the disease by observing the power and the balance of the round and the square.

The power and balance, the circle and the square, in accordance with other texts (Suwen chapter 17, Huainanzi chapter 5), represent the movements of the four seasons. They are perceived above all at the pulse.

In spring, *yang qi* start to rise up. They are active, but not yet established. They must be supple to prevent the tightening up of movement, and are described in terms of the circular nature of a compass (*gui* 規).

In summer, the movements outwards and upwards reach their height and their limit, and the abundance within form is completed. This is represented by the square (*ju* 矩), which delimits the richness of forms.

In autumn, a state of equilibrium becomes firmly established, and things are tightly controlled to prepare for the point at which the *yinyang* movement turns back on itself. This is represented by the central bar of the scales (*heng* 衡), and describes the moving point of balance between the two scales.

In winter, life turns inwards to protect itself. There is a proper assessment of what is essential for managing life and preserving its energy. This is represented by the power and heaviness of the weights on the scales (*quan* 權) which assess and make judgements.

In the body, the pulses indicate the advance or retreat of the seasons. We know what is controlling the illness when we know which movement is speeding up and which is slowing down.

203. 觀 浮 沈 滑 澀 而 知 病 所 生 以 治
guan fu chen hua se er zhi bing suo sheng yi zhi

He perceives what has caused the disease by taking the pulse on the proximal and distal positions, and by observing whether they are superficial or deep, slippery or choppy.

This describes the examination of the qualities of the pulses to determine the characteristic features of the illness, and the affected organ where the illness has started and begins to show itself.

204. 無 過 以 診 則 不 失 矣
wu guo yi zhen ze bu shi yi

His treatment is then faultless, because his diagnosis never errs.

Looking at the complexion, listening to the sounds and palpating the pulse, together with questioning the patient, form the four aspects of traditional diagnosis.

205. 故 曰 病 之 始 起 也 可 刺 而 已 其 盛 可 待 衰 而 已
gu yue bing zhi shi qi ye ke ci er yi qi sheng ke dai shuai er yi

Thus it is said: When illness first appears, we need only needle, and it is gone. If it has developed further, we must wait until it decreases and then it will cease.

In any treatment, if we have overlooked the first signs which would have made it possible to intervene gently with quick results, it is better to wait for an opportune moment. If not, we run the risk of harming recovery by carrying out interventions which weaken more than they help the natural movement. In this way we avoid treating when the illness is at its height to ensure that we do not disturb the patient's balanced *qi* by interventions foreign to it, as they focus on dispelling the harmful energies.

206. 故因其輕而揚之因其重而減之因其衰而彰之
gu yin qi qing er yang zhi yin qi zhong er jian zhi yin qi shuai er zhang zhi
So, faced with a benign situation, drain; faced with a serious situation, reduce; faced with a situation in decline, restore resplendence.

A superficial illness can easily be treated using a rapid dispersal technique and by inducing a sufficient amount of sweating. In serious cases, the harmful energies that have accumulated must be released, the blocked pathways unblocked and the perverse internal *qi* eliminated.

Once imbalance has been reduced, or alternatively, (in another possible interpretation of the text), if the correct (balanced) *qi* are deficient, tonification is carried out, giving strength back to the *qi* and vigour to the blood. In addition to using needles and remedies, recovery can be aided by prescribing an appropriate food regime based upon the selection of tastes.

207. 形不足者溫之以氣
xing bu zu zhe wen zhi yi qi
If the deficiency is in the body, warm by the *qi*.

The *qi* which pass through the density of the flesh and warm it are principally *yang* defensive *qi*. By enabling the defensive *qi* to circulate freely once more and by restoring their power, the body will be well-maintained and function with ease. If the body is not functioning properly it is not enough to nourish it with tastes; we should remember here that 'if the body is nourished by tastes, ...the *qi* produce the body' (cf. Suwen chapter 5 above).

208. 精不足者補之以味
jing bu zu zhe bu zhi yi wei
If the deficiency is in the essences, tonify by the tastes.

When there are insufficient essences, strength is given back to the *zang* by providing them with tastes, which are the raw material for the development of essences.

209. 其高者因而越之
qi gao zhe yin er yue zhi
If the upper areas are affected, expel towards the outside.

When the upper part of the body is affected, the perverse is 'chased away' (*yue* 越) by expelling what is blocking the body through vomiting.

210. 其下者引而竭之
qi xia zhe yin er jie zhi
If the lower areas are affected, drain to empty them.

When the stomach and the lower abdomen are affected, the stagnant dampness is 'pulled' (*yin* 引) downwards by using diuretics or laxatives.

211. 中滿者瀉之於內
zhong man zhe xie zhi yu nei
If the centre is congested, disperse internally.

Here the centre is a description of what is deep within, rather than of the middle heater. The knots and congestion are serious and cannot be unravelled by discharging from above or below. They must be dispersed by acting upon subtle mechanisms which relieve and release, and work upon the digestion and interconnections. It is by eliminating harmful energies that balance can be re-established.

212. 其 有 邪 者 漬 形 以 為 汗
    qi you xie zhe zi xing yi wei han
In case of perverse *qi*, flush the body by profuse sweating.

Harmful energies which are not firmly attached to the flesh can be removed by abundant sweating, and pushed outwards by hot vapours.

213. 其 在 皮 者 汗 而 發 之
    qi zai pi zhe han er fa zhi
If at the level of the skin, induce an out break of sweat.

Sweating helps to expel the harmful energies which have installed themselves on the outside, on the surface of the body.

214. 其 慓 悍 者 按 而 收 之
    qi piao han zhe an er shou zhi
If lively and active, compress and gather in.

Agitated *qi* can be calmed by massage to help restore normal circulation and maintain internal balance.

215. 其 實 者 散 而 瀉 之
    qi shi zhe san er xie zhi
If full, spread and disperse.

Yang fullness is diffused (*san* 散) and *yin* fullness is dispersed (*xie* 寫).

216. 審 其 陰 陽 以 別 柔 剛
    shen qi yin yang yi bie rou gang
***Yin* and *yang* are examined to differentiate between the soft and the hard.**

What we understand as *yinyang* at the level of heaven/earth, becomes what is hard and soft (*gang rou* 剛柔), and expresses the equivalent of these phenomena on earth. The hard here describes the rise in power of harmful *qi*, causing *yang* illnesses, and the soft the absence of balanced *qi*, causing *yin* illnesses.

217. 陽 病 治 陰 陰 病 治 陽 定 其 血 氣 各 守 其 鄉
yang bing zhi yin yin bing zhi yang ding qi xue qi ge shou qi xiang
In *yang* disease treat by the *yin*, and in *yin* disease treat by the *yang*; stabilize blood and *qi* and ensure that each remains within its own territory.

The balance between the meridians, between blood and *qi*, is re-established by using methods which cross *yin* and *yang* and create exchanges between them. Here, the 'territory' (*xiang* 鄉) describes the blood/*qi* relationship in each meridian. If this is controlled, it prevents the *qi* from encroaching upon the blood or the blood upon the *qi*.

218. 血 實 宜 決 之 氣 虛 宜 掣 引 之
xue shi yi jue zhi qi xu yi che yin zhi
If there is an excess of blood, a way must be cleared, and if there is an emptiness of *qi*, they must be drawn in and guided.

An excess of blood causes blockage and stagnation, and the restriction must be forced open. Deficiency of *qi* is a progressive reduction in the correct amount of *qi* in the body. When *qi* is insufficient in certain areas of the vital circulation, *qi* which are still active and plentiful 'elsewhere' are drawn towards these areas. *Qi* is encouraged to be circulated and distributed in a balanced way through needling or massage.

REFERENCES

Granet, Marcel, *La Droite et la Gauche en Chine, Etudes Sociologiques sur la Chine* (Paris, PUF, 1953)

Karlgren (translator) *Hong Fan: Shujing (Book of Documents)* (Göteborg, 1950)

Larre, Claude and Elisabeth Rochat de la Vallée, *Les 11 Premiers Chapitres, Par Cinq* (Paris, Maisonneuve, 1993)

Larre, Claude and Elisabeth Rochat de la Vallée, *The Heart in Lingshu chapter 8* (London: Monkey Press, 2000)

Larre, Claude and Elisabeth Rochat de la Vallée, *The Lung* (London: Monkey Press, 2001)

Larre, Claude and Elisabeth Rochat de la Vallée, *Rooted in Spirit* (New York: Station Hill Press, 1995)

Larre, Claude and Rochat de la Vallée, Elisabeth, *The Seven Emotions* (London: Monkey Press, 1996)

Major, John, *Heaven and Earth in Early Han Thought: Chapters 3, 4 and 5 of Huainanzi* (Albany: State University of New York Press, 1993)

Rochat de la Vallée, Elisabeth, *A Study of Qi* (London: Monkey Press, 2006)

Rochat de la Vallée, Elisabeth, *Wu Xing* (London: Monkey Press, 2009)